Praise Him

Vivien Hibbert

ISBN 978-0-9786908-0-9

Library of Congress Control Number 2007902513

Printed in the U.S.A. by
Morris Publishing
3212 East Highway 30
Kearney, NE 68847
1-800-650-7888

Acknowledgements

I have come to understand that even as Christ is my supreme and eternal love, yet family and friends are our greatest treasures on earth. They are the jewels that build dignity into our hearts. Our most valuable friends are those who inspire us to run harder after Christ and grow deeper in His grace; they join their voices with ours as we sing songs of praise and live to bring honor to Him. Each of the following has brought the light of Christ to my life—they have contributed to the anthems of my personal praises. I acknowledge them now with great fondness:

Very special thanks to Rebecca, my sister, friend and assistant. Your hunger for the deep things of God makes me ever richer. May we always run together! I wouldn't get anything done without your help and encouragement.

One of the greatest reasons I have to praise the Lord is for the lives of Stephen, Meg and Chad. It is a joy to watch you grow into adults of exceptional character.

Huge thanks to the board, staff and all past, present and future students of The Worship Arts Conservatory.

Thank you Yvonne; Dan and Sarah; Brad, Julie and all of Origins Community; Corky, Sharon and all The Fellowship; Don and Connie; Sister Baker; Jo; David and Elaine; Steve and Mary; Women's Ministry at POTL; Martha and Steve V; Marianne; Irene; Pat F; Gordon; Mark; Geir and Elin; PJ and Liz; Ken and Elizabeth; Carl and Yvonne, Teresa and Linda, and all my friends at Dance Camp, Symposium, YWAM Denver, IWI and CWI.

Rita Springer; Alberto and Kimberly Rivera—your songs walk with me in the dark and hold me near to the Father.

In prosperity, our friends know us;
in adversity, we know our friends
John Churton Collins.

Contents

Preface

"Alleluia! For the Lord God Omnipotent reigns!
Let us be glad and rejoice and give Him glory,
for the marriage of the Lamb has come,
and His wife has made herself ready."
Rev. 19:6-7

This book of praise is my answer to one of the most difficult seasons in my life. I had no voice to vindicate myself; no means to seek justice; no power to change the position I found myself in. While writing these pages, I learned to live a life of praising God in the face of overwhelming personal pain. The simplicity and supremacy of praise is my sole response to this present suffering. Praise is the altar I leave here to mark the difficult journey I am on.

The final part of this book was written during a prayer journey to Italy. While traveling to Rome, Assisi, Florence and Pisa, I saw some of the most outstanding churches, architecture, sculptures, paintings and monuments to mankind's greatness, creativity and spiritual magnificence that have ever been produced. Saint Peter's Basilica is thought to be one of the most impressive churches in the entire world, and the sublime paintings and sculptures of Michelangelo and other Renaissance artists are simply breath-taking. The catacombs bear witness to the purity and clarity of Christian faith from the first centuries. The hilltop city of Assisi causes one to be lost in time, as it stands bathed in the mystical setting sun of Umbria.

It occurred to me that as stunning as these cities and their treasures are, yet the Lord has called us to craft even more magnificent masterpieces of praise in our own hearts and before His throne.

The Psalmist calls on us to create glorious praises in the face of all enemies and all nations as he addresses us with this appeal:

Ps 66:2 *Sing out the honor of His name; Make His praise glorious.*

In this verse the Creator of all creators asks us to "make" beauty before Him with songs of praise and the sincere offerings of our hearts. We are called upon to become creative masters of exquisite praises. I believe that the Lord delights in our earnest gifts of worship even more than we might take pleasure in the magnificence of the artistic works seen in Italy.

It is said that Michelangelo's stunning *David* was sculpted out of a discarded, inferior block of marble. Now the Lord takes our once useless and inadequate lives and forms the most priceless treasures in us. He assists us and provides the tools and inspiration as we create masterful praises for our Creator. He equips us to chisel songs of praise out of our most desperate days.

Whether you are walking through dark valleys or gazing at wonders both natural and created, allow your heart to soar with abundant praise.

Come with me through these pages and meditate on the glorious splendor of His majesty and on His wondrous works (Ps. 145:5). Fill your mouth with words and songs that remember the wonders of His great goodness. Think of ways to declare His excellencies from day to day and from generation to generation.

As you do this, you will find the creative ability to make magnificent praises for your King that are worthy of their own place in God's eternal records.

I have opened every chapter with one of the great anthems of worship from the Book of Revelation. Allow these perfect songs of praise to inspire you.

It is my prayer for you, that through this little book, you will be led to your own hymns of praise and, ultimately, to a profound and genuine encounter with God. In this place of meeting, He will form Himself in you and prepare you for eternity with your Bridegroom King. Praise Him in every circumstance and He will beautify you and fill you with His glory!

There are a few scriptures that have been used more than once. When a particular verse was crucial in more than one list, I have used it again.

I have compiled these lists from many Bible translations. Most often, however, I have used the New King James Version, New International Version and New Living Translation.

Every one of these lists is inadequate and incomplete. Fill in the gaps with your own praises and your own discoveries of His wonders from the Word.

Chapter One

Praise Him

"You are worthy, O Lord,
To receive glory and honor and power;
For You created all things,
And by Your will they exist and were created."
Rev. 4:11

We Are Priests Of Praise

All true praise and worship must begin and remain centered on God and His absolute worthiness to receive all honor and glory.

There are no techniques for worship, here; no instructions for the praise band—just a number of doorways for you to open to the vast realms of praise that await us all. In fact, the first and greatest responsibility for every Believer is to be a priest of praise. There are so many important things we can do in service of our gracious Father, but nothing quite holds the imperative to serve Him as His personal ministers of praise and worship—through all seasons of our lives; in all places; at all times; and with all our heart, soul, mind, and strength.

I think most of us have grown up with the understanding that "priests" or "ministers" are those who have dedicated their lives and profession to service of God and the Church. The concept of priesthood throughout the New Testament, however, is not that of a professional ministry class, but it is God's expectation for every Believer:

1Pet. 2:5, 9 *You also, as living stones, are being built up a spiritual house, a holy priesthood, to offer up spiritual sacrifices acceptable to God through Jesus Christ.*

But you are a chosen generation, a royal priesthood, a holy nation, His own special people, that you may proclaim the praises of Him who called you out of darkness into His marvelous light.

There are no verses in the New Testament that use the word "priest" to describe a profession, except in connection with priests of the Old Covenant. The New Testament also describes Christ's priestly ministry among His Church. In fact, He is our High Priest. When Christ came to earth, the whole function and ministry of the priesthood changed. The priestly ministry of Christ superseded the priesthood of the Old Covenant. The changing law brought with it an entirely new priesthood, of which we are now a part:

Heb. 7:12 *For the priesthood being changed, of necessity there is also a change of the law.*

My point is simply to call attention to the fact that every Believer has responsibilities and ministry duties that remain unexplored. Not only have we been granted a new law and a new High Priest (Christ), but He now calls us to operate in this priestly role as holy and royal people, and excellent ministers of this New Covenant.

So many Christians expect their pastor to do all the work in the church. They somehow have the mistaken notion that they "pay" for the pastor to take care of their every need. They expect their worship leaders and teams to "produce" the presence of God for them, and to sing the songs that *they* like. They come to church in order to have their needs met, not to minister to God and others. The Church will never grow to her full potential under this sort of administration. However, if every Believer catches this principle—that it is their responsibility to function as a priest and to live in the presence of God as a lifestyle—then the lost will be saved in much greater numbers (as more people will be reaching out to them) and the day of His glory will be upon us. I am convinced that this principle of the "priesthood of praisers" would revolutionize the Church, and ultimately the world.

Genuine and passionate praise is the key to evangelism, global revival and the maturity of the Church—the Bride of Christ. The nations are waiting for the Church to become ignited with fervent worship. As the

Lord is lifted up (not only on the cross, but in praise), He will draw all men and all nations to Himself.

One of the primary functions of the Old Testament priests was to offer sacrifices. This is no longer necessary, as Christ became our perfect sacrifice. No more blood sacrifice is needed for the salvation of man, and now this duty of ministering *spiritual* sacrifices has been conferred upon every Christian.

As far as I can see, there are seven spiritual sacrifices that we have the privilege of offering throughout our lives, and whenever we gather for corporate worship:

- The sacrifice of joy—Ps. 27:6
- The sacrifice of a broken spirit—Ps. 51:16-17
- The sacrifice of righteousness—Ps. 51:19
- The sacrifice of praise—Ps. 54:6; Heb. 13:15
- The sacrifice of thanksgiving—Ps. 116:17
- The sacrifice of fellowship and sharing—Heb. 13:16
- The sacrifice of our bodies—Rom. 12:1

As God's personal ministers, we have a great and honorable work to do when we come to our worship services—the primary ministers of worship are *not* the worship team, but the congregation. The worship team is simply there to assist and serve the people as they function in their glorious work of praise and worship.

We Are Kings Of Praise

Not only are we all priests before the Lord, but we are also kings:

Rev. 5:10 *And have made us kings and priests to our God; And we shall reign on the earth."*

We are to carry upon our lives the dignity and nobility that comes from our royal birth, and the holiness and piety that is expected from a true priest.

6

Peter tells us that we are *holy* and *royal* priests. We have heard so much over the years about our call as a holy priesthood, and very little about our function as royal priesthood.

This means that we have been invited to boldly draw near to the very throne of our King and carry out the prescribed duties of a priest (Heb. 4:16). The worship service is no place for pouting or observing; it is our place of sacrifice and kingly ministry. We are both royal ministers before God, and royal administrators of His Kingdom in all the earth.

It doesn't matter if you are young or old, rich or poor, wise or simple, strong or weak, confined to a bed, or locked in prison, confident or shy—we are all called to stand before Him as His personal priests and dedicated ministers.

From 1Pet. 2:5, 9 we can see seven descriptions or attributes of God's priests:

1. God's Priests are **living** stones
2. God's Priests are a **spiritual** house
3. God's Priests are a **chosen** generation
4. God's Priests are a **royal** priesthood
5. God's Priests are a **holy** nation
6. God's Priests are a **special people**
7. God's Priests are **praisers** of God

In this little book I am only focusing on the issue of our priestly praise ministry. I am going to attempt to show you the scope of God's request made to every Christian—that we would minister praises before Him. In my opinion, our present praise offerings in most of our churches are scant compared to what the Lord has in mind.

As we can see from the list above, we are living; we are spiritual; we have been chosen; we have been adorned in His royalty; we have been challenged to holiness; we are very special—specifically so that we would *proclaim His praises* in all the earth. When you read this verse, it begins with the various descriptions of us and our qualifications to be His priests, but it ends with Him, the things He has done and the reason for this ministry—so that we can touch the nations on His behalf. Praise is not simply a vertical expression, but it is the means by which that the Lord has chosen to fill the earth with His glory. In the end, it is *all* about Him; it is *all* about His glory; it is *all* about His kingdom.

It is the Lord who has taken every one of us from the darkness of our own destruction and willfulness to the light of His glory and countenance. We, who do not deserve His favor, have been wooed by His love into the position of His special friends and priests. Now He is delighted to use us as priests to show His character and grace to the entire world. This can never happen by evangelism and missions, alone. Praise is the missing key to establishing His kingdom throughout our cities nations.

We Are Ambassadors Of Praise

The praises we have been called to offer are not simply to be spoken or sung, but the Word says that we are to *proclaim* these praises. Some translations include the concept that we are to make known the wonderful virtues and excellencies of God in the earth. This definitely calls us to more than a duty of singing a few songs on Sunday morning and going home. This verse implies the requirement of a life's worth of action and demonstration on our part.

The Greek word for *proclaim,* is *exaggello* (Strong's # 1804), which means:

> To tell
> To make known by praising or celebrating
> To celebrate

Exaggello comes from two Greek words:

Ex meaning: the point where action or motion proceeds; out of.

Aggelos meaning: to bring forth tidings; angel or messenger, envoy, one who is sent; to accompany something to a place, to bring to a destination, to attach one's self as an attendant, to lead, to move.

8

We are called to be God's royal envoys and messengers who have become one with the praises we speak or sing. We have become the message to such a degree that we accompany those praises wherever they are sent. The life and essence of every worshiper, and the glory of God that is in them, accompanies the praises and establishes God's holy, royal kingdom in that very place. When we praise Him, we are like the heavenly host in Luke 2:13-14

And suddenly there was with the angel a multitude of the heavenly host praising God and saying "Glory to God in the highest, And on earth peace, goodwill toward men!"

The great host of angels accompanied the good news of Jesus' birth and filled the place with praises that resounded throughout heaven and earth, filling time and eternity. Now we have been called to accompany the message of praise and declare His eternal Kingdom from one end of the earth to the other.

When Jesus came in the flesh, He used angels to accompany the message of His arrival. In these last days, He wants to use His holy, royal priests to accompany the message of His presence in the earth and His return as Conquering King!

Paul also speaks of this principle as He writes to the Corinthians:

2Cor. 2:14 *But praise be to God who makes us strong to overcome in Christ, and makes clear through us in every place the value of the knowledge of him.*

Now read this same verse in the New Living Testament:

But thanks be to God, who made us his captives and leads us along in Christ's triumphal procession. Now wherever we go he uses us to tell others about the Lord and to spread the Good News like a sweet perfume.

Our praise-filled lives are like a sweet perfume—we affect every place we go and every person we come in contact with.

He has commissioned us to accompany the message of praise that we sing and speak. Something of our relationship with the Lord and His authority working in and through us affects the atmosphere. We are the royal ambassadors of our King. Through us, and our praises, He unleashes His dominion and makes way for His presence in the earth.

I know that He is able to do all of this on His own. I realize that all the earth is the Lord's (Ps. 24:1) without our help or permission, but in His infinite wisdom He has directed us to minister on His behalf, and rule with Him in kingdom matters of heaven and earth.

As with all royal communiqués, the message is more important than the messenger.

We Create A Throne Of Praise

Another important principle in praise is the *enthroning* principle. The Lord *inhabits*, or *dwells* in; or is *enthroned* upon our praise:

Ps. 22:3 *But You are holy, Enthroned in the praises of Israel.*

In other words, our praises become a throne for our King. All the authority and majesty of the King is present in our most humble offerings. When you stop to think about that, it is awesome! He could choose to sit on some glorious planet somewhere that He created just for Himself—with sights and sounds that far exceed anything we could ever imagine. Instead, He is seated with us as we minister praises before Him. He has chosen us. *We* are the objects of His longing. *We* are His preferred dwelling place. When we praise Him, we become the sweetest and most desirable place for the Lord to dwell.

As you worship, you can sing praises over nations, cities and governments. You have the royal authority to proclaim God's dominion and kingdom in places far and near simply by lifting your voice and giving glory and honor to your King. He who is enthroned in your praise will make Himself known through you. His glory will fill the earth as His glory fills and flows through the proclaiming praisers.

As Legal Maxim has said:

The Church is the mansion-house of the Omnipotent God.

Summary

Everyone who is a believer in Christ has been called to bring passionate and genuine praise before the Lord. You have also been called to participate with Him as He establishes His sovereign territory in every place through your declarations of His greatness. Not only do we establish His presence in the place of our praise, but we also accompany the message with His Divine authority overlaying our humble offerings.

He wants us to be known for our praise, our righteousness, and our love. In the last days the praises of God's people will be like beautiful flowers springing up before all nations (Is. 61:11).

This book is simply a small sampling of the call to praise Him found in every book of the Bible. (In most of these instances I have only listed one Scripture as a key verse for that particular point. Where other verses might help with the overall understanding of a specific point, I have included them).

Chapter Two

Praise Him For His Wonderful Name

Who will not fear you, O Lord, and bring glory to your name?
For you alone are holy. All nations will come and worship before you,
for your righteous acts have been revealed.
Rev. 15:4

His Names

Gen. 2:4	Praise Him our Lord God
Gen. 14:18-20	Praise Him our God Most High
Gen. 15:2	Praise Him our Master, Lord
Gen. 17:1-2	Praise Him our Almighty, All Sufficient
Gen. 16:13	Praise Him our God who Sees
Gen. 22:13-14	Praise Him our Provider
Gen. 49:24	Praise Him our Mighty One
Ex. 3:14	Praise Him our Self-Existent One
Ex. 15:3	Praise Him our Warrior
Ex. 15:22-26	Praise Him our Healer and Restorer
Ex. 17:8-16	Praise Him our Banner
Ex. 34:14	Praise Him our Jealous God
Lev. 20:8	Praise Him our Sanctifier
Dt. 4:24	Praise Him our Consuming Fire
Dt. 32:8	Praise Him our Most High
Jud. 6:4	Praise Him our Peace
Ruth 3:9-4:14	Praise Him our Kinsman-Redeemer
2Sam. 22:2	Praise Him our Rock
2Sam. 22:29	Praise Him our Keeper
Ps. 2:2	Praise Him our Anointed One
Ps. 3:3	Praise Him our shield
Ps. 7:8	Praise Him our Judge
Ps. 7:9	Praise Him our Righteous One
Ps. 10:16	Praise Him our King

Ps. 18:2	Praise Him our Horn of Salvation
Ps. 22:19	Praise Him our Strength
Ps. 23	Praise Him our Shepherd
Ps. 27:1	Praise Him our Light and Salvation
Ps. 29:3	Praise Him our God of glory
Ps. 32:7	Praise Him our Hiding place
Ps. 94:22	Praise Him our Defender
Ps. 121:5	Praise Him our Keeper
Pr. 8	Praise Him our wisdom
Pr. 18:10	Praise Him our Strong Tower
Song of Sol.	Praise Him our Bridegroom
Song 2:1	Praise Him our Rose of Sharon
Song 2:1	Praise Him our Lily of the Valley
Is. 1:24	Praise Him our Lord of Hosts
Is. 7:14	Praise Him our Immanuel (Matt. 1:23)
Is. 9:6	Praise Him our Counselor
Is. 9:6	Praise Him our Everlasting Father
Is. 9:6	Praise Him our Prince of Peace
Is. 25:4	Praise Him our Refuge
Is. 43:3	Praise Him our Savior
Is. 44:6	Praise Him our First and Last
Is. 51:15	Praise Him our Lord of Hosts
Is. 53:3	Praise Him our Man of Sorrows
Is. 59:20	Praise Him our Redeemer
Is. 64:8	Praise Him our Potter
Jer. 23:5-6	Praise Him our Righteousness
Lam. 3:22-23	Praise Him our Faithful One
Ez. 48:35	Praise Him our God who is There
Hos. 2:16, 19-20	Praise Him our Husband
Micah 5:2	Praise Him our ruler
Hag. 2:7	Praise Him our Desire of Nations
Zech. 6:12	Praise Him our Branch
Mal. 3:3	Praise Him our Refiner
Mal. 4:2	Praise Him our Sun of Righteousness
Matt. 8:20	Praise Him our Son of Man
Matt. 9:27	Praise Him our Son of David
Lu. 1:31	Praise Him our Jesus
Lu. 1:78	Praise Him our Dayspring
Lu. 4:23	Praise Him our Physician
Jn. 1:1	Praise Him our Word

Jn. 1:29, 36	Praise Him our Lamb of God
Jn. 1:32	Praise Him our Dove
Jn. 1:38	Praise Him our Rabbi
Jn. 1:41	Praise Him our Messiah
Jn. 6:14	Praise Him our Prophet
Jn. 7:37-39	Praise Him our Water
Jn. 10:7-9	Praise Him our Door
Jn. 14:17	Praise Him our Spirit of Truth
Jn. 14:26	Praise Him our Comforter (2Cor. 1:3)
Acts 2:1-2	Praise Him our Wind
Rom. 8:15	Praise Him our Abba
Rom. 15:12	Praise Him our Root of Jesse
1Cor. 15:45	Praise Him our Last Adam
Eph. 1:22	Praise Him our Head
Eph. 2:20	Praise Him our Cornerstone
1Tim. 2:5	Praise Him our Mediator
1Tim. 6:15	Praise Him our Potentate
Heb. 4:14	Praise Him our Great High Priest
Heb. 12:2	Praise Him our Author and Finisher of Faith
Heb. 12:29	Praise Him our Fire
1Pet. 2:25	Praise Him our Bishop of our Souls
1Pet. 5:10	Praise Him our God of all Grace
2Pet. 1:19	Praise Him our Daystar
1Jn. 2:1	Praise Him our Advocate
3Jn. 1:4, 8	Praise Him our Truth
Rev. 1:8	Praise Him our Alpha and Omega
Rev. 1:17	Praise Him our First and Last
Rev. 3:14	Praise Him our Faithful and True Witness
Rev. 3:14	Praise Him our Beginning
Rev. 5:5	Praise Him our Lion of Judah
Rev. 7:2	Praise Him our Living God
Rev. 15:3	Praise Him our King of saints
Rev. 19:3	Praise Him our Word of God
Rev. 19:11	Praise Him our Faithful and True
Rev. 19:13	Praise Him our Word
Rev. 19:16	Praise Him our King of Kings
Rev. 19:16	Praise Him our Lord of Lords
Rev. 22:16	Praise Him our Morning Star

Is. 11:2	Praise Him—the Spirit of the Lord
Is. 11:2	Praise Him—the Spirit of Wisdom
Is. 11:2	Praise Him—the Spirit of Understanding
Is. 11:2	Praise Him—the Spirit of Counsel
Is. 11:2	Praise Him—the Spirit of Might
Is. 11:2	Praise Him—the Spirit of Knowledge
Is. 11:2	Praise Him—the Spirit of the Fear of the Lord

Gen. 1:1	Praise Him—Elohim, our Creator
Gen. 18:3	Praise Him—Adonai, our Master
Gen. 2	Praise Him—Jehovah, our Eternal God of covenant
Gen. 17:1-2	Praise Him—Jehovah-El Shaddai, our Supplier
Gen. 22:14	Praise Him—Jehovah-Jireh, our Provider
Ex. 15:22-26	Praise Him—Jehovah-Rapha, our Healer
Ex. 17:15-16	Praise Him—Jehovah-Nissi, our Banner, victory
Ex. 31:13	Praise Him—Jehovah-M'kadesh, our Sanctifier
Jud. 6:23-24	Praise Him—Jehovah-Shalom, our Peace
Jer. 23:5-6	Praise Him—Jehovah-Tsidkenu, our Righteousness
Ps. 23	Praise Him—Jehovah-Rohi, our Shepherd
Ez. 48:35	Praise Him—Jehovah-Shammah, our God who is there, present with us. Our abiding presence

Jn. 10:1-7	Praise Him—Jesus is the Door of the Sheep
Jn. 10:10-14	Praise Him—Jesus is the Good Shepherd
Heb. 13:20	Praise Him—Jesus is the Great Shepherd
1Pet. 5:4	Praise Him—Jesus is the Chief Shepherd

Jn. 8:51-59	Praise Him—He said, "I Am"
Jn. 6:35-58	Praise Him—He said, "I am the Bread of Life"
Jn. 8:12	Praise Him—He said, "I am the Light of the world"
Jn. 10:1-18	Praise Him—He said, "I am the Good Shepherd"
Jn. 11:17-27	Praise Him—He said, "I am the Resurrection and the Life
Jn. 14:1-14	Praise Him—He said, "I am the Way, the Truth and the Life"
Jn. 15:1-17	Praise Him—He said, I am the True Vine"

Ex. 3:6, 15-16	Praise Him—the God of Abraham (Gen. 26:24)
Ex. 3:6, 15-16	Praise Him—the God of Isaac (Gen. 46:1)
Ex. 3:6, 15-16	Praise Him—the God of Jacob (Gen. 49:24)
2Ki. 2:14	Praise Him—the God of Elijah
2Ki. 20:5	Praise Him—the God of David
Dan. 3:28-29	Praise Him—the God of Shadrach, Meshach, and Abed-Nego
Dan. 6:26	Praise Him—the God of Daniel
Acts. 5:30	Praise Him—the God of our fathers (2Chr. 20:6)
Gen. 24:3	Praise Him—the God of heaven and earth
Ex. 5:1	Praise Him—the God of Israel (Jer. 31:1)
Num. 16:22	Praise Him—the God of the spirits (life) of all flesh
Dt. 10:17	Praise Him—the God of gods
Dt. 32:4	Praise Him—the God of truth
1Sam. 17:45	Praise Him—the God of the armies of Israel
2Sam. 5:10	Praise Him—the God of hosts
2Sam. 22:3	Praise Him—the God of my strength
1Chr. 16:35	Praise Him—the God of my salvation (Ps. 51:14)
2Chr. 32:19	Praise Him—the God of Jerusalem
Ps. 4:1	Praise Him—the God of my righteousness
Ps. 29:3	Praise Him—the God of glory
Ps. 42:8	Praise Him—the God of my life
Ps. 59:10, 17	Praise Him—the God of mercy
Ps. 109:1	Praise Him—the God of my praise
Is. 30:18	Praise Him—the God of justice
Is. 54:5	Praise Him—the God of the whole earth
Jer. 51:56	Praise Him—the God of recompense
Matt. 22:32	Praise Him—the God of the living
Rom. 3:29	Praise Him—the God of the Jews and the Gentiles
Rom. 15:5	Praise Him—the God of patience
Rom. 15:13	Praise Him—the God of hope
Rom. 15:33	Praise Him—the God of peace
2Cor. 1:3	Praise Him—the God of all comfort
2Cor. 13:11	Praise Him—the God of love
Eph. 1:17	Praise Him—the God of our Lord Jesus Christ
1Pet. 5:10	Praise Him—the God of all grace
Rev. 22:6	Praise Him—the God of the holy prophets

Ps. 68:5	Praise Him—He is the Father of the fatherless
Rom. 15:6	Praise Him—He is the Father of our Lord Jesus Christ
2Cor. 1:3	Praise Him—He is the Father of mercies
Eph. 1:17	Praise Him—He is the Father of glory
Eph. 4:6	Praise Him—He is the Father of all
Heb. 12:9	Praise Him—He is the Father of our spirits
Jas. 1:17	Praise Him—He is the Father of lights

Matt. 1:1	Praise Him—He is the Son of David, the son of Abraham
Matt. 8:20	Praise Him—He is the Son of Man
Matt. 8:29	Praise Him—He is the Son of God (Mt. 14:33; 16:16)
Lu. 1:32	Praise Him—He is the Son of the Highest
Lu. 8:228	Praise Him—He is the Son of the Most High God

Rom. 8:2	Praise Him—He is the Spirit of Life
Rom. 8:15	Praise Him—He is the Spirit of Adoption
Rom. 1:4	Praise Him—He is the Spirit of Holiness
Jn. 16:13	Praise Him—He is the Spirit of Truth
Zech. 12:10	Praise Him—He is the Spirit of Grace
Rom. 8:26-27	Praise Him—He is the Spirit of Supplication
Is. 11:2	Praise Him—He is the Spirit of Wisdom
2Cor. 4:13	Praise Him—He is the Spirit of Faith
1Pet. 4:14	Praise Him—He is the Spirit of Glory

The Affects Of His Name

Num. 6:27	Praise Him for His name is upon His people and through His name He blesses us (1Chr. 16:2)
Dt. 12:11	Praise Him for His name abides with us (Dt. 16:11; 26:2)
Jud. 13:18	Praise Him for His name is a secret
1Chr. 13:6	Praise Him for His name is proclaimed (Dt. 32:3; Ex. 33:19)
1Chr. 17:24	Praise Him for His name is magnified forever
1Chr. 29:13	Praise Him for His name is glorious (Dt. 28:58)
2Chr. 14:11	Praise Him for His name is a help in warfare
Neh. 9:5	Praise Him for His name is above all blessing and praise

Ps. 20:1	Praise Him for His name is our defense
Ps. 20:5	Praise Him for His name is our banner
Ps. 8:1, 9	Praise Him for His name is excellent
Ps. 20:7	Praise Him for His name is remembered in battle
Ps. 30:4	Praise Him for His name is remembered
Ps. 44:5	Praise Him for His name is powerful against every enemy
Ps. 54:6	Praise Him for His name is good
Ps. 66:2	Praise Him for His name is honorable
Ps. 72:17	Praise Him for His name is forever (Ps. 135:13)
Ps. 75:1	Praise Him for His name is near
Ps. 76:1	Praise Him for His name is great
Ps. 86:9	Praise Him for His name is glorified in all the nations
Ps. 86:11	Praise Him for His name is to be feared
Ps. 96:2	Praise Him for His name is blessed
Ps. 96:8	Praise Him for His name is worthy of all glory
Ps. 99:3	Praise Him for His name is awesome
Ps. 111:9	Praise Him for His name is holy and awesome
Ps. 119:55	Praise Him for His name is with you in the night
Ps. 119:132	Praise Him for His name is to be loved
Ps. 135:3	Praise Him for His name is pleasant
Ps. 148:13	Praise Him for His name is exalted
Ps. 149:3	Praise Him for His name is worthy of dance and song
Pr. 18:10	Praise Him for His name is a strong tower
Song 1:3	Praise Him for His name is like ointment
Is. 9:6	Praise Him for His name is Wonderful
Is. 26:8	Praise Him for His name is the desire of my soul
Is. 52:6	Praise Him for His name is known
Ps. 64:6	Praise Him for His name is known to His enemies
Jer. 10:6	Praise Him for His name is great in might
Hos. 12:5	Praise Him for His name is memorable
Zech. 14:9	Praise Him for His name is the only one
Mal. 1:11	Praise Him for His name is great among the nations
Mal. 1:14	Praise Him for His name is feared among the nations
Matt. 1:21, 25	Praise Him for His name is Jesus
Matt. 12:21	Praise Him for His name is trustworthy (Ps. 33:21)
Mk. 6:14	Praise Him for His name is famous
Jn. 12:28	Praise Him for His name is, and will be glorified
Jn. 20:31	Praise Him for His name is life
Rom. 9:17	Praise Him for His name is declared in all the earth

Rom. 15:9	Praise Him for His name is our reason to sing
Eph. 1:21	Praise Him for His name is far above all principality and power and might and dominion, and every name that is named, not only in this age but also in that which is to come. (Phil. 2:9)
2Thess. 1:12	Praise Him for His name is glorified in us
Heb. 1:4	Praise Him for His name is more excellent than the angels' names
Ps. 54:1	Praise Him for His name is able to save (Rom. 10:13)
Ps. 118:10	Praise Him for His name is able to destroy nations
Ps. 124:8	Praise Him for His name is able to help
Acts 3:16	Praise Him for His name is able to make you strong
Acts 4:30	Praise Him for His name is able to bring signs and wonders
Acts 16:18	Praise Him for His name is able to command demons
1Cor. 6:11	Praise Him for His name is able to justify
1Jn. 2:12	Praise Him for His name is able to forgive sins
Rev. 3:5	Praise Him for He will announce our names before the Father
Rev. 3:12	Praise Him for He will write His name on us (Rev. 14:1; 22:4)
Is. 49:16	Praise Him for He will write our names on His hands
Rev. 19:12	Praise Him for He has a name that no one knows
Matt. 18:20	Praise Him for He is with us when we gather in His name
Matt. 21:9	Praise Him for He comes in the name of the Lord
Jn. 14:26	Praise Him for He has sent us the Holy Spirit in His name
Mk. 16:17	Praise Him for His name gives us power over demons
Mk. 16:17	Praise Him for His name gives us ability to speak in tongues

He Gives Us Power Through His Name

Dt. 10"8	Praise Him for we can bless in His name
Dt. 18:5, 7	Praise Him for we can stand before Him and minister or serve in His name forever
1Sam. 17:45	Praise Him for we can confront enemies in His name (2Chr. 14:11)
1Chr. 16:10	Praise Him for we can glory in His name
1Chr. 16:29	Praise Him for glory is due to His name
2Chr. 33:4	Praise Him for His name is in Jerusalem forever
Ps. 7:17	Praise Him for we can sing songs to His name (Ps. 69:30)
Ps. 83:18	Praise Him for His name stands alone
Is. 12:4	Praise Him for we can call upon His name (1Ki. 18:24; Ps. 86:7; 116:4, 13, 17)
Matt. 28:19	Praise Him for can we make disciples in His name
Mk. 13:13	Praise Him for you will be hated by all for His name's sake (Lu. 21:12, 17)
Lu. 24:47	Praise Him for repentance and forgiveness of sins is preached in His name to all nations
Jn. 1:12	Praise Him for we can become children of God when we believe in His name
Jn. 14:14	Praise Him for we can ask anything in His name and He will do it (15:16; 16:23-24)
Jn. 20:31	Praise Him for we can have life in His name
Acts 2:21	Praise Him for we are saved when we call on His name (Acts 4:12)
Acts 2:38	Praise Him for we are baptized in His name
Acts 3:6	Praise Him for the sick can rise up and walk in His name (Acts 4:10)
Acts 5:41	Praise Him for we are counted worthy to suffer for His name (Acts 9:16)
Acts 9:29	Praise Him for we can preach boldly in His name
Acts 10:43	Praise Him for through His name, whoever believes in Him will receive forgiveness of sins (1Jn. 2:12)
Acts 15:14	Praise Him for He has made us a people in His name
Acts 15:17	Praise Him for we are called by His name
Rom. 9:17	Praise Him for we declare His name in all the earth
Rom. 10:13	Praise Him for we can call on His name and be saved

Rom. 15:9	Praise Him for we can sing to His name among the Gentiles
1Cor. 6:11	Praise Him for we are washed, justified and sanctified in His name
Phil. 2:10	Praise Him for every knee will bow at His name
Col. 3:17	Praise Him for we do everything in His name
2Thess. 1:12	Praise Him for His name is glorified in us and we in Him
Heb. 13:15	Praise Him for we give thanks to His name
Jas. 5:14	Praise Him for we can anoint the sick with oil in His name
1Jn. 2:12	Praise Him for we are forgiven in His name
1Jn. 3:23	Praise Him for we can believe in His name (1Jn. 5:13)
3Jn. 1:7	Praise Him for we are sent out in His name
Rev. 2:13	Praise Him for we can hold on to His name
Rev. 19:3	Praise Him for His name will be written on our foreheads

Chapter Three

Praise Him For His Magnificent Person

After these things I heard a loud voice of a great multitude
in heaven, saying, "Alleluia! Salvation and glory and honor and power
belong to the Lord our God!"
Rev. 19:1

He Is Magnificent

Ps. 139:7-10	Praise Him - the omnipresent One (Jer. 23:23-24; Ac. 17:24-28)
Ps. 33:6-9	Praise Him - the Omnipotent One (Gen. 1; Mk. 10:27; Rev. 19:6)
Job 37:16	Praise Him - the Omniscient One (Ps. 147:5; 1 Jn. 3:20)
Ps. 90:2, 4	Praise Him - the Eternal One (Ps. 102:24-27)
Mal. 3:6	Praise Him - the Unchangeable One
Ps. 145:17	Praise Him - the Righteous One
Ps. 103:8	Praise Him - the Merciful One
Dt. 7:9	Praise Him - the Faithful One
1Jn. 4:8	Praise Him - the Loving One
Jer. 10:10-16	Praise Him - the Living One
Is. 42:1	Praise Him - the Elect One
Is. 6:3	Praise Him - the Holy One
Zeph. 3:5	Praise Him - the Just One
Is. 43:13	Praise Him for He existed before the day
Pr. 8:23	Praise Him for He existed before the earth
1Pet. 1:20	Praise Him for He existed before the foundations of the earth
Col. 1:15	Praise Him for He existed before God made anything
Rev. 13L8	Praise Him for He was slain before the foundation of the earth

Ps. 46:10	Praise Him for He comes quietly
Is. 40:11	Praise Him for He comes gently
Is. 53:7	Praise Him for He comes meekly
Acts 2:2	Praise Him for He comes suddenly
	(Num. 16:42; Matt. 3:17; Acts 22:6)
Hos. 6:3	Praise Him for He comes like rain
Ps. 18:10	Praise Him for He comes like wind
	(Ps. 104:3; Song 4:16; Acts 2:2)
Is. 57:15	Praise Him for He inhabits eternity
Eccl. 3:11	Praise Him for He puts eternity into our hearts
Is. 40:12	Praise Him for He measured the waters
Is. 40:12	Praise Him for He measured the heavens
Is. 40:12	Praise Him for He measured the dust of the earth
Is. 40:12	Praise Him for He weighed the mountains and hills
Is. 40:13	Praise Him for He does not need to be taught
Is. 40:14	Praise Him for He does not need counsel
Is. 40:14	Praise Him for He does not need instruction
Is. 40:14	Praise Him for He does not need instruction in justice
Is. 40:14	Praise Him for He does not need instruction in knowledge and understanding
Is. 40:18, 25	Praise Him for there is no one like Him
Is. 40:26	Praise Him for He created all things and knows them by name
Is. 40:28	Praise Him for He created the ends of the earth
Is. 40:28	Praise Him for He never faints or gets weary
Is. 43:11	Praise Him for there is no Savior beside the Lord
Is. 44:6, 8	Praise Him for there is no God beside our God
Is. 45:6, 21	Praise Him for there is none beside Him
Matt. 3:17	Praise Him for He is a God who speaks
1Thess. 1:10	Praise Him for He is resurrected

Matt. 6:9	Praise Him—His name is holy
Matt. 6:10	Praise Him—His kingdom will come
Matt. 6:10	Praise Him—His will is accomplished in the earth
Matt. 6:10	Praise Him—His will is accomplished in heaven
Matt. 6:11	Praise Him—He gives us our daily needs
Matt. 6:12	Praise Him—He forgives us for all our sins
Matt. 6:12	Praise Him—He helps us to forgive others
Matt. 6:13	Praise Him—He leads us away from temptation
Matt. 6:13	Praise Him—He delivers us from evil
Matt. 6:13	Praise Him—the kingdom, power and glory all belong to Him

He Is Eternal, Immortal, Invisible And Wise (1Tim. 1:17)

Dt. 33:7	Praise Him—He is an eternal God (Rom. 16:26)
Rom. 6:23	Praise Him—He gives us eternal life (1Tim. 6:12)
2Cor. 4:18	Praise Him—He offers us eternal things (2Cor. 5:1)
Eph. 3:11	Praise Him—He accomplished His eternal purpose through Christ
2Tim. 2:10	Praise Him—He makes us participants in His eternal glory (2Cor. 4:17; 1Pet. 5:10)
Heb. 5:9	Praise Him—He is the author and source of our eternal salvation
Heb. 6:20	Praise Him—He is our eternal High Priest
Heb. 9:12	Praise Him—He has secured our eternal redemption through His blood
Heb. 9:14	Praise Him—He is an eternal Spirit
Heb. 9:15	Praise Him—He has given us an eternal inheritance
Heb. 13:20	Praise Him—He has made an eternal covenant
1Pet. 1:23	Praise Him—His word is eternal and living
2Pet. 1:11	Praise Him—His kingdom is eternal
Rev. 14:6	Praise Him—His gospel is eternal
1Tim. 6:16	Praise Him—He alone is immortal (Rom. 1:23)
Col. 1:15	Praise Him—He is the visible image of the invisible God (Heb. 11:27)
Rom. 1:20	Praise Him—we can see His invisible qualities (His eternal power and divine nature) through His creation

| Col. 1:16 | Praise Him—He created visible and invisible things |

Jude 1:25	Praise Him—He alone is wise (Rom. 16:27; 1Tim. 1:17)
1Cor. 3:20	Praise Him—He knows all the thoughts of the wise
Ps. 19:7	Praise Him—He makes even the simple man wise
1Cor. 1:27	Praise Him—He chooses foolish things to shame the wise
1Cor. 3:19	Praise Him—He finds the wise things of the world to be foolish
Pr. 3:35	Praise Him—He gives the wise an inheritance of glory

He Is A Living God Who Brings Us To Life

Jn. 6:57	Praise Him—He is the Living Father
Dt. 5:26	Praise Him—He is our Living God (Ps. 42:2; 84:2)
Rev. 1:18	Praise Him—He is the Living One
Hos. 1:10	Praise Him—we are sons of the Living God (Rom. 9:26)

| Jer. 2:13 | Praise Him—He is our fountain of living waters |
| Jn. 7:38 | Praise Him—we have rivers of His living water flowing out of our hearts |

| 1Pet. 2:4 | Praise Him—He is the living Stone |
| 1Pet. 2:5 | Praise Him—He has made us into living stones |

| Jn. 6:51 | Praise Him—He is our living bread |
| Ps. 145:16 | Praise Him—He satisfies the desire of every living thing |

| Acts 7:38 | Praise Him—He gives us living words |
| 1Pet. 1:23 | Praise Him—He has given us a living Word (1Jn. 1:1) |

| Heb. 10:19-22 | Praise Him—He has opened for us a living way |
| 1Pet. 1:3 | Praise Him—He has given us a living hope |

| Jn. 14:10 | Praise Him—He is living in us |
| Acts 17:28 | Praise Him—we are living in Him |

Job 12:9-10	Praise Him—He holds the life of every living thing
Rom. 12:1	Praise Him—we offer our bodies as living sacrifices
2Cor. 6:16	Praise Him—we are the temples of the living God
Rev. 4:6	Praise Him—He is surrounded by four living creatures

There is Nothing Too Difficult For Him

Jer. 32:17, 27	Praise Him—there is nothing too difficult for Him
Gen. 1:1-31	Praise Him—He can create every thing
Job 12:10	Praise Him—He can hold every breath
Ps. 139:1-4	Praise Him—He can account for every detail
Lu. 12:7	Praise Him—He can number every hair
Ps. 107:9	Praise Him—He can fill every emptiness
Jn. 12:32	Praise Him—He can persuade every heart
1Cor. 10:13	Praise Him—He can ease every temptation
Rev. 5:9	Praise Him—He can redeem every sinner
Matt. 12:31	Praise Him—He can forgive every sin
1Chr. 22:18	Praise Him—He can defeat every enemy (Ps. 91:3)
Ps. 118:10-12	Praise Him—He can destroy every army
Matt. 17:20	Praise Him—He can move every mountain
Is. 40:4	Praise Him—He can exalt every valley
Is. 54:17	Praise Him—He can silence every tongue
Jn. 8:10	Praise Him—He can mute every accusation
Ps. 27:1, 3	Praise Him—He can conquer every fear
Is. 53:5	Praise Him—He can feel every pain
Matt. 9:35	Praise Him—He can heal every sickness
Dan. 2:22, 28	Praise Him—He can explain every mystery
Lu. 1:37	Praise Him—He can overcome every difficulty
Ps. 22:5	Praise Him—He can relieve every disappointment
1Ki. 1:29	Praise Him—He can resolve every problem
Pr. 16:1	Praise Him—He can answer every question
2Cor. 10:5	Praise Him—He can pull down every stronghold
Mk. 1:32-34	Praise Him—He can banish every demon
Rom. 8:15, 21	Praise Him—He can shatter every bondage
Is. 61:1	Praise Him—He can unlock every prison
Phil. 4:19	Praise Him—He can meet every need
1Pet. 5:7	Praise Him—He can handle every concern
Ps. 145:16	Praise Him—He can satisfy every desire
Jn. 4:13-14	Praise Him—He can quench every thirst

2Cor. 1:3-5	Praise Him—He can comfort every sorrow
Zeph. 3:5	Praise Him—He can correct every injustice
Pr. 2:9	Praise Him—He can right every wrong
Ps. 18:28	Praise Him—He can light every darkness
Lu. 15:11-32	Praise Him—He can restore every prodigal
Is. 61:1-4	Praise Him—He can mend every brokenness
Ps. 55:22	Praise Him—He can carry every burden
Rev. 21:4	Praise Him—He can wipe every tear
Pr. 15:3	Praise Him—He can see every place
Is. 59:1	Praise Him—He can hear every cry
Ps. 28:7	Praise Him—He can help every situation
Ps. 46:10	Praise Him—He can still every heart
Acts 2:17	Praise Him—He can nurture every dream
Ps. 50:10	Praise Him—He can finance every enterprise
Pr. 3:5-6	Praise Him—He can guide every pathway
Ps. 139:16	Praise Him—He can control every destiny
Eccl. 3:1	Praise Him—He can utilize every purpose
Ps. 102:12	Praise Him—He can reach every generation
Ps. 98:2	Praise Him—He can touch every nation
Jn. 3:16	Praise Him—He can love every soul
1Cor. 15:51-55	Praise Him—He can annihilate every death

There Is None To Compare With Him

Ps. 89:6	Praise Him for no one can be compared to Him (Is. 40:18; 46:5; 50:8)
Lu. 13:18, 20	Praise Him for no kingdom can be compared to His kingdom
Rom. 8:18	Praise Him for there is no suffering that can be compared with the glory that He will reveal in us

Chapter Four

Praise Him For His Radiant Beauty

Worthy is the Lamb who was slain
To receive power and riches and wisdom
And strength and honor and glory and blessing!
Rev. 5:12

He Is Beautiful In Appearance

Is 53:2	Praise Him for when He came to us, there was no beauty in Him to attract us to Him
Dan. 10:6	Praise Him for His face is like lightning
Dan. 10:6	Praise Him for His body is like beryl
Dan. 10:6	Praise Him for the sound of His words is like the voice of a multitude
Rev. 1:13	Praise Him for He is clothed down to the feet
Rev. 1:13	Praise Him for He is girded about the chest with a band of gold
Rev. 1:14	Praise Him for His head and hair are white like wool and snow
Rev. 1:14	Praise Him for His eyes are a flame of fire
Rev. 1:15	Praise Him for His feet are like brass (Rev. 2:18)
Rev. 1:15	Praise Him for His voice is like many waters
Rev. 1:16	Praise Him for His hand holds seven stars
Rev. 1:16	Praise Him for His mouth is like a sword
Rev. 1:16	Praise Him for His face is as bright as the sun
Rev. 4:3	Praise Him for His face is like a precious and beautiful stone

Song 5:16	Praise Him for He is lovely in every way
Song 1:16	Praise Him for He is handsome
Song 2:14	Praise Him for His face is lovely
Song 3:6	Praise Him for He smells like myrrh, frankincense and all beautiful spices
Song 5:10	Praise Him for He is better than ten thousand others
Song 5:11	Praise Him for His head is like the finest gold
Song 5:11	Praise Him for His hair is wavy and very black
Song 6:5	Praise Him for His hair is like a flock of goats
Song 5:12	Praise Him for His eyes are like doves beside the water—they are like jewels
Song 5:13	Praise Him for His cheeks are like spices and herbs
Song 5:13	Praise Him for His lips are like perfumed lilies
Song 5:13	Praise Him for His breath is like myrrh
Song 5:14	Praise Him for His hands are like rods of gold set with jewels
Song 5:14	Praise Him for His body is like carved ivory inlaid with sapphires
Song 5:15	Praise Him for His legs are pillars of marble set on bases of the finest gold
Song 5:15	Praise Him for His countenance is as strong as the cedars of Lebanon
Song 5:16	Praise Him for His mouth is sweet
Song 6:6	Praise Him for His teeth are like white newly washed sheep—they are perfectly matched and none are missing
Song 6:7	Praise Him for His cheeks are like pomegranates

He Shares His Beauty With Us

Song 5:16	Praise Him for He is altogether lovely
Song 4:7	Praise Him for He finds us beautiful and spotless
Song 6:4-5, 9	Praise Him for He finds us as beautiful as Tirzah
1Chr. 16:29	Praise Him for His holiness makes us beautiful (Ps. 96:9; 110:3)
Ps. 33:1	Praise Him for He finds our praise to be beautiful
Ps. 50:2	Praise Him for He calls us (Zion), "the perfection of beauty, the joy of the whole earth"
Ps. 90:7	Praise Him for His beauty is upon us
Is. 61:3	Praise Him for He gives us beauty instead of ashes

Is. 52:1	Praise Him for He has given us beautiful garments
Is. 52:7	Praise Him for He declares that our feet are beautiful
Ez. 16:1-14	Praise Him for He has made us completely beautiful
Ps. 45:11	Praise Him for He greatly desires our beauty
Ps. 27:4	Praise Him for He shows us His beauty
Eccl. 3:11	Praise Him for He makes everything beautiful
Ps. 96:6	Praise Him for strength and beauty are in His sanctuary
Ps. 147:1	Praise Him for He finds our praises to be beautiful
Ps. 149:4	Praise Him for He beautifies the humble with salvation
Ez. 16:6-7	Praise Him for He takes us out of our struggles and shame, and makes us beautiful
Ez. 16:8	Praise Him for He covers us with His wing and makes us beautiful
Ez. 16:9	Praise Him for He washes and anoints us to make us beautiful
Ez. 16:10	Praise Him for He clothes us with embroidered cloth, sandals, fine linen and silk to make us beautiful
Ez. 16:11	Praise Him for He adorns us with ornaments, puts bracelets on our wrists, and a chain on our necks to make us beautiful
Ez. 16:12	Praise Him for He puts a jewel in our nose, earrings in our ears and a crown on our head to make us beautiful
Ez. 16:13	Praise Him for He has made us exceedingly beautiful and has called us to royalty
Ez. 16:14	Praise Him for He has made our beauty known among the nations. He has made our beauty perfect because of His glory and splendor which He has imparted to us.
1Pet. 3:3-5	Praise Him for He causes us to have the unfading beauty of a gentle and quiet spirit. This beauty is precious to the Lord
Rev. 21:1-2	Praise Him for He has prepared a beautiful place for us to dwell with Him forever

His Voice

Gen. 3:8-10	Praise Him when you hear His voice from the garden
Ex. 3:4	Praise Him when you hear His voice from the fire
Num. 7:89	Praise Him when you hear His voice from the mercy seat
1Sam. 3:3-4	Praise Him when you hear His voice from your bed
Job 38:1	Praise Him when you hear His voice out of the whirlwind
Is. 6:8	Praise Him when you hear His voice from the throne
Is. 66:6	Praise Him when you hear His voice from the temple
Ez. 1:28	Praise Him when you hear His voice from the brightness of glory
Joel 2:11	Praise Him when you hear His voice from before His army
Joel 3:16	Praise Him when you hear His voice from Zion
Jn. 5:28	Praise Him when you hear His voice from the grave
Acts 9:3-4	Praise Him when you hear His voice from the light
Jn. 10:4	Praise Him when you know His voice
Ex. 19:5	Praise Him when you obey His voice
Ps. 138:4	Praise Him when you hear the words of His mouth
Ps. 106:12	Praise Him when you believe the words of His mouth
2Sam. 22:14	Praise Him when you hear the thunder of His voice
1Ki. 19:12	Praise Him when you hear His still, small voice
Job 37:2-4	Praise Him when you hear His majestic voice
Ps. 47:5	Praise Him when you hear the shout of His voice
Ps. 68:33	Praise Him when you hear His mighty voice
Ps. 29:3	Praise Him when His voice is over the waters
Ps. 29:4	Praise Him when His voice is powerful
Ps. 29:5	Praise Him when His voice breaks the cedars
Ps. 29:7	Praise Him when His voice divides the flames
Ps. 29:8	Praise Him when His voice shakes the wilderness
Ps. 29:9	Praise Him when His voice makes the deer give birth
Ps. 29:9	Praise Him when His voice strips the forests bare
Ps. 46:6	Praise Him when His voice melts the earth
Is. 42:13	Praise Him when His voice cries out like a warrior

Jer. 10:13	Praise Him when His voice fills the heavens with water
Jer. 25:30	Praise Him when His voice is a roar
Hos. 11:10	Praise Him when His voice is like a roaring lion
Rev. 1:10	Praise Him when His voice is like a trumpet
Rev. 1:15	Praise Him when His voice is like many waters

His Eyes

Ps. 33:18	Praise Him for His eyes are on all those who fear Him
Ps. 34:15	Praise Him for His eyes are on the righteous
Ps. 66:7	Praise Him for His eyes are on the nations
Ps. 11:4	Praise Him for His eyes examine us all (Pr. 5:21)
Pr. 15:3	Praise Him for His eyes see everything
Zech. 4:10	Praise Him for His eyes search throughout the earth (1Chr. 16:9)
Zech. 12:4	Praise Him for His eyes watch over Judah (praise)
Pr. 22:12	Praise Him for His eyes watch over knowledge
Ps. 32:8	Praise Him for He guides you with His eye
Ps. 33:18	Praise Him for He guards you with His eye

His Arms

Jer. 32:17	Praise Him for He creates with His arm (Jer. 27:5)
Ps. 77:15	Praise Him for He redeems us with His arm
Ps. 89:10	Praise Him for He scatters our enemies with His arm
Ps. 98:1	Praise Him for He gains the victory with His arm
Is. 51:5	Praise Him for He judges with His arm
Jer. 32:21	Praise Him for He rescued Israel with His arm
Is. 52:10	Praise Him for He saves the nations with His arm
Ps. 89:21	Praise Him for He strengthens us with His arm
Is. 53:1	Praise Him for He reveals His greatness with His arm
Mk. 10:16	Praise Him for He gathers us in His arms

His Hands

Ps. 48:10	Praise Him when He has righteousness in His hand
Ps. 145:16	Praise Him when He satisfies you from His hand
Ps. 104:28	Praise Him when He provides for you with His hand
Ps. 139:10	Praise Him when He leads you with His hand
Is. 49:2	Praise Him when He hides you in His hand
Is. 49:16	Praise Him when He engraves you on His hand
Is. 51:16	Praise Him when He covers you with His hand
Ez. 37:1	Praise Him when He comes over you with His hand
Matt. 8:3	Praise Him when He heals you with His hand
Ps. 21:8	Praise Him when He ministers justice with His hand
Is. 40:12	Praise Him when He measures the waters, the earth and the heavens with His hand
1Ki. 8:24	Praise Him when He fulfills His promises with His hand
Ps. 37:24	Praise Him when He upholds you with His hand
Ps. 73:23	Praise Him when He holds you with His hand
Is. 62:3	Praise Him when He holds you as a crown of glory in His hand
Dan. 5:23	Praise Him when He holds your breath in His hand
Pr. 21:1	Praise Him when He holds your heart in His hand
Eccl. 9:1	Praise Him when He holds the righteous, the wise and all their works in His hand
Pr. 30:4	Praise Him when He holds the wind in His hand
Hab. 3:4	Praise Him when He holds His power and light in His hand
Rev. 1:16	Praise Him when He holds seven stars in His hand
Rev. 14:14	Praise Him when He holds a sharp sickle in His hand
Jn. 3:35	Praise Him when He has all things in His hand

His Wings

Ps. 63:7	Praise Him when you are hidden under the shadow of His wings (Ps. 91:1)
Mal. 4:2	Praise Him when you are hidden under His healing wings
Ps. 17:8	Praise Him when He watches over you as the apple of His eye under His wings
Is. 40:31	Praise Him when He lifts you up with eagle's wings

Dt. 32:10-11	Praise Him when He carries you on His eagle wings
Ps. 61:4	Praise Him when He gives you a place of refuge under His wings (Ps. 57:1)
Ez. 16:8	Praise Him when He covers your shame with His wings
Matt. 23:37	Praise Him when He gathers you with His protecting wings
Ps. 63:7	Praise Him when He gives you a song from under His wings
Ps. 91:1	Praise Him when you find the secret place under the shadow of His wings
Ps. 36:7	Praise Him when you put your trust under the shadow of His wings
Ps. 57:1	Praise Him when you find a refuge under the shadow of His wings
Ps. 63:7	Praise Him when you rejoice and sing under the shadow of His wings
Song 2:3	Praise Him when you sit under His shadow
Is. 32:2	Praise Him when you are protected under His shadow
Is. 49:2	Praise Him when He hides and polishes you under the shadow of His hand (Is. 51:16)
Hos. 14:7	Praise Him for you will be revived under His shadow
Jas. 1:17	Praise Him for there is no change or shadow of turning in him

His Royal Clothing

Ps. 93:1	Praise Him for He is clothed with majesty
Ps. 104:1	Praise Him for He is clothed with honor
Ps. 104:2	Praise Him for He is clothed with light
Ps. 65:6	Praise Him for He is clothed with power and strength (Ps. 93:1)
Is. 59:17	Praise Him for He is clothed with righteousness
Is. 59:17	Praise Him for He is clothed with justice
Is. 59:17	Praise Him for He is helmeted with salvation
Is. 59:17	Praise Him for He is cloaked with zeal
Is. 6:1	Praise Him for the train of His robe is long enough to fill the temple

His Royal Crowns (And The Crowns Of The Church)

Ps. 8:5	Praise Him for He is crowned with glory (Heb. 2:7, 9)
Ps. 8:5	Praise Him for He is crowned with honor (Heb. 2:7, 9)
Is. 62:3	Praise Him for He is crowned with the Church (Zech. 9:16)
Matt. 27:29	Praise Him for He is crowned with thorns
Rev. 6:2	Praise Him for He is crowned as a conqueror
Ps. 103:4	Praise Him for He has crowned us with love and tender mercies
Pr. 4:9	Praise Him for He has crowned us with wisdom
Pr. 12:4	Praise Him for He has crowned us with honor
Pr. 14:18	Praise Him for He has crowned us with knowledge
Pr. 14:24	Praise Him for He has crowned us with riches
Pr. 17:6	Praise Him for He has crowned us with grandchildren
Is. 28:5	Praise Him for He has crowned us with His glory (Is. 62:3; 1Pet. 5:4)
Eph. 1:3	Praise Him for He has crowned us with every spiritual blessing
Phil. 4:1	Praise Him for He has crowned us with those we influence for the Gospel (1Thess. 2:19)
1Thess. 2:19	Praise Him for He has crowned us with rejoicing
2Tim. 4:8	Praise Him for He has crowned us with righteousness (Pr. 16:31)
Jas. 1:12	Praise Him for He has crowned us with life (Rev. 2:10)

His Royal Throne

Ps. 93:2	Praise Him for His throne is established from time immemorial
Ps. 22:3	Praise Him for He is enthroned in the praises of His people
Rev. 5:13	Praise Him for He is enthroned in heaven (Ps. 11:4)
Ps. 9:4, 7	Praise Him for He judges from His throne
Is. 6:1	Praise Him for His throne is high and lifted up
Matt. 25:31	Praise Him for His throne is filled with glory

35

Heb. 1:8	Praise Him for His throne is forever and ever
Ps. 89:14	Praise Him for n His throne is founded on righteousness and justice (Ps. 97:2)
Is. 16:5	Praise Him for His throne is established in mercy
Dan. 7:9	Praise Him for His throne is a fiery flame
Rev. 4:3	Praise Him for His throne is surrounded by a rainbow
Rev. 4:5	Praise Him for His throne is surrounded by lightening, thunder and voices
Rev. 4:8	Praise Him for His throne is surrounded by four creatures who continuously cry praises to Him
Rev. 4:10	Praise Him for His throne is surrounded by 24 elders who bow before Him and cast their crowns before Him
Rev. 5:11-12	Praise Him for His throne is surrounded by a hundred million worshiping angels—plus thousands upon thousands
Is. 40:22	Praise Him for He sits enthroned on the circle of the earth

His Kingdom

Ps. 45:6	Praise Him for righteousness is the scepter of His kingdom
Ps. 103:19	Praise Him for His kingdom rules over all
Ps. 145:12-13	Praise Him for His kingdom is full of glory and majesty
Dan. 4:3	Praise Him for His kingdom is everlasting
Lu. 1:33	Praise Him for His kingdom has no end
Matt. 3:2	Praise Him for the kingdom of God is at hand
Matt. 6:13	Praise Him for the kingdom is completely His
Matt. 13:24	Praise Him for the kingdom of heaven is like a man who sowed good seed in his field
Matt. 13:33	Praise Him for the kingdom of heaven is like leaven
Matt. 13:44	Praise Him for the kingdom of heaven is like treasure hidden in a field
Matt. 13:45	Praise Him for the kingdom of heaven is like a merchant seeking beautiful pearls

Matt. 13:47	Praise Him for the kingdom of heaven is like a dragnet that was cast into the sea and gathered some of every kind
Matt. 13:52	Praise Him for the kingdom of heaven is like a householder who brings out of his treasure things new and old
Matt. 18:23	Praise Him for the kingdom of heaven is like a certain king who wanted to settle accounts with his servants
Matt. 20:1	Praise Him for the kingdom of heaven is like a landowner who went out early in the morning to hire laborers for his vineyard
Matt. 22:2	Praise Him for the kingdom of heaven is like a certain king who arranged a marriage for his son
Matt. 25:1	Praise Him for the kingdom of heaven is like ten virgins who took their lamps and went out to meet the bridegroom
Matt. 25:14	Praise Him for the kingdom of heaven is like a man traveling to a far country who called his servants and delivered his goods to them

Matt. 6:33	Praise Him for we are seeking His kingdom
Matt. 13:11	Praise Him for we can know the mysteries of His kingdom
Jas. 2:5	Praise Him for He has promised to give us the kingdom
Matt. 16:19	Praise Him for He has given us the keys of the kingdom
Matt. 18:3	Praise Him for we must enter His kingdom as a child
Matt. 24:14	Praise Him for the gospel of the kingdom will be preached in all the world before He comes again
Matt. 25:34	Praise Him for the kingdom is our inheritance
Lu. 12:32	Praise Him for it is the Father's pleasure to give us the kingdom
Lu. 17:21	Praise Him for the kingdom is within us
Jn. 3:3	Praise Him for we can see the kingdom when we are born again
Jn. 3:5	Praise Him for we can enter the kingdom of God when we are born of the water and the Spirit

1Cor. 4:20	Praise Him for the kingdom is not just talk, but it is God's power
Col. 1:13	Praise Him for He has rescued us from the kingdom of darkness and has brought us into the kingdom of His Son
1Thess. 2:12	Praise Him for He calls us into His kingdom and glory
Heb. 12:28	Praise Him for His kingdom cannot be shaken
Rev. 1:6	Praise Him for He has made us kings and priests of His kingdom (Rev. 5:10; 1Pet. 2:9)
Rev. 11:15	Praise Him for the kingdoms of this world have become His kingdoms and He will reign forever and ever
Rom. 14:17	Praise Him for His kingdom is righteousness
Rom. 14:17	Praise Him for His kingdom is peace
Rom. 14:17	Praise Him for His kingdom is joy
Is. 9:7	Praise Him for the increase of His kingdom—His government, peace and justice—will know no end
Lu. 1:22	Praise Him for His reign and His kingdom will never end
Ps. 107:27	Praise Him for His years will never end
Matt. 6:29	Praise Him for there is nothing that man can make that is as beautiful as the things He has made
1Pet. 1:24-25	Praise Him for although all beauty will fade, yet His Word will last forever
Ex. 33:18-34:8	Praise Him when you see Him (Lev. 9:23-24)
Song 2:8	Praise Him when you hear Him
Ps. 34:8	Praise Him when you taste Him
Ps. 45:8	Praise Him when you smell Him
Mk. 3:10	Praise Him when you touch Him

Chapter Five

Praise Him For His
Mighty Power

We give You thanks, O Lord God Almighty,
The One who is and who was and who is to come,
Because You have taken Your great power and reigned.
Rev. 11:17

He Is Mighty

Lu. 1:49	Praise Him for He is mighty
Ps. 45:3	Praise Him for He is the mighty One (Ps. 50:1)
Neh. 9:32	Praise Him for He is the mighty God (Is. 9:6)
Ps. 24:8	Praise Him for He is mighty in battle
Is. 42:13	Praise Him for He is like a mighty man
Acts 2:2	Praise Him for He is a mighty wind
Ps. 68:33	Praise Him for He has a mighty voice
Dt. 3:24	Praise Him for He has a mighty hand
Ps. 89:10, 13	Praise Him for He has a mighty arm (Is. 63:12)
Ps. 106:8	Praise Him for He has mighty power (Eph. 1:19)
Job 9:4	Praise Him for He has mighty strength
Job 36:5	Praise Him for He has mighty strength of understanding
Dt. 3:24	Praise Him for He does mighty deeds
Ps. 150:2	Praise Him for He does mighty acts (Ps. 106:2; 145:4, 12)
Jer. 33:3	Praise Him for He does great and mighty things
Dan. 4:3	Praise Him for He does mighty wonders
Micah. 7:15	Praise Him for He does mighty miracles
Mk. 6:2	Praise Him for He does mighty works
2Cor. 13:3	Praise Him for He is mighty in you (Col. 1:29)
Eph. 3:16	Praise Him for He gives you mighty inner strength

2Sam. 22:50-51	Praise Him for He is a tower of salvation
Ps. 61:3	Praise Him for He is a strong tower (Pr. 18:10)
Ps. 144:2	Praise Him for He is a high tower

He Is A Mighty Creator

| Heb. 1:10 | Praise Him for He laid the foundations of the earth (Job 38:4, 6) |
| Heb. 1:3 | Praise Him for He upholds all things by the word of His power |

Gen. 1:1	Praise Him for He created the heavens and the earth
Gen. 1:3	Praise Him for He created the light
Gen. 1:4-5	Praise Him for He created the night and the day
Gen. 1:6-8	Praise Him for He created the sky
Gen. 1:9-10	Praise Him for He created the earth and the seas
Gen. 1:11-12	Praise Him for He created the grass, plants and trees
Gen. 1:14-18	Praise Him for He created the sun and moon
Gen. 1:20-22	Praise Him for He created the fish and birds
Gen. 1:24-25	Praise Him for He created the animals on the earth
Gen. 1:26-27	Praise Him for He created man and woman
Gen. 1:28-30	Praise Him for He gave mankind dominion over all His creation
Gen. 1:31	Praise Him for everything He created was good

Job 38:5, 18	Praise Him for He measured the earth
Job 38:8, 11	Praise Him for He birthed the sea and set its borders
Job 38:12	Praise Him for He commands the morning
Job 38:16	Praise Him for He knows the depths of the sea
Job 38:17	Praise Him for He knows the gates of death
Job 38:19	Praise Him for He knows where light and darkness come from
Job 38:22	Praise Him for He has a treasure house for snow and hail where they are designed and stored
Job 38:24	Praise Him for He sets the course for light and wind
Job 38:25	Praise Him for He sets the course for lightening
Job 38:26-27	Praise Him for He waters all the earth and causes things to grow
Job 38:28-29	Praise Him for He created all the waters and ice

Job 38:31-33	Praise Him for He commands the stars and constellations
Job 38:34-35	Praise Him for He commands the rain and lightening with His voice
Job 38:36	Praise Him for He is the source of all wisdom
Job 38:37-38	Praise Him for He can count the clouds and start the rain when the earth is hardened
Job 38:39-41	Praise Him for He can hunt like a lion and the raven
Job 39:1-4	Praise Him for He knows when all the creatures give birth and how they grow
Job 39:5-18	Praise Him for He created the wild animals to be free and He designed their intricate ways
Job 39:25	Praise Him for He put strength in the horse and clothed its neck with beauty and thunder (power) —He filled the horse with courage in war
Job 39:26-30	Praise Him for the hawk and the eagle fly and live by His design
Job 40:9	Praise Him for His arm is strong and His voice is like thunder
Job 40:10	Praise Him for He is robed with majesty and splendor; glory and beauty
Job 40:15-24	Praise Him for He created huge animals and gave them strength—only God can come near them
Job 41:1-34	Praise Him for He has all power over the devil
Jer. 31:35	Praise Him for He gives us the sun to light the day
Jer. 31:35	Praise Him for He gives us the moon and stars as lights in the night
Jer. 31:35	Praise Him for He stirs the seas so that the waves roar
Col. 1:16	Praise Him for by Him all things were created in heaven and in earth—visible and invisible, thrones, principalities and powers
Heb. 3:4	Praise Him for He built all things
Heb. 11:3	Praise Him for He framed the worlds with His Word
Ps. 33:6	Praise Him for He created the heavens with His Word and with the breath of His mouth
Ps. 33:7	Praise Him for He gathered the oceans and set their borders

Ps. 33:9	Praise Him for when He spoke the world began—it appeared at His command
Ps. 4:19	Praise Him for He is a faithful Creator
Ps. 33:8	Praise Him all the earth, and stand in awe of Him
Ps. 5:7	Praise Him with deepest awe
Lu. 5:26	Praise Him when you are filled with awe (Lu. 7:16)
Ps. 19:1	Praise Him for the heavens declare the glory of God and the skies show His handiwork
Ps. 97:6	Praise Him for the heavens declare His righteousness And all nations see His glory (Ps. 50:6)

He Is Mighty In Knowledge

Ps. 147:4	Praise Him for He knows every star by name and put them in their place
Ps. 103:14	Praise Him for He knows how we are formed
Ps. 91:14	Praise Him for He knows your name
Dt. 2:7	Praise Him for He knows when you are in the wilderness, and how to provide for you
Lu. 12:7	Praise Him for He knows every hair on your head (Matt. 10:29-31)
Ps. 44:21	Praise Him for He knows the secrets of your heart
Ps. 94:11	Praise Him for He knows your thoughts
Ps. 139:1	Praise Him for He knows everything about you
Ps. 139:2	Praise Him for He knows when you sit down and when you rise up
Ps. 139:3	Praise Him for He knows all your ways (Job 23:10)
Ps. 37:18	Praise Him for He knows all your days
Ps. 139:4	Praise Him for He knows all your words before you speak them
Dan. 2:22	Praise Him for He knows everything that is in darkness
Nah. 1:7	Praise Him for He knows those who trust Him

His Might Fills The Earth

Ps. 24:1	Praise Him for the earth is the Lord's, and all its fullness (1Cor. 10:26, 28)
Ps. 33:5	Praise Him for the earth is full of His goodness
Ps. 72:19	Praise Him for the earth is full of His glory (Is. 6:3; Hab. 2:14)
Ps. 104:24	Praise Him for the earth is full of His possessions (creatures, substance)
Ps. 119:64	Praise Him for the earth is full of His mercy
Is. 11:9	Praise Him for the earth will be full of the knowledge of the Lord
Hab. 3:3	Praise Him for the earth is full of His praise
Ps. 29:4	Praise Him for His voice is full of majesty
Ps. 48:10	Praise Him for His right hand is full of righteousness
Ps. 78:38	Praise Him for He is full of compassion (Ps. 111:4)
Ps. 86:15	Praise Him for He is full of mercy, grace, love and truth (Jn. 1:14)
Acts 2:2	Praise Him—He makes us full of joy in His presence
Acts 6:3; 11:24	Praise Him—He makes us full of the Holy Spirit
Acts 6:3	Praise Him—He makes us full of wisdom
Acts 6:5	Praise Him—He makes us full of faith
Acts 6:5	Praise Him—He makes us full of power
Acts 9:36	Praise Him—He makes us full of good works
Rom. 15:14	Praise Him—He makes us full of goodness
Rom. 15:14	Praise Him—He makes us full of knowledge

He Has Given Us His Might

Ps. 93:4	Praise Him for He is mightier than the noise of many waters
1Cor. 1:25	Praise Him for His weakness is stronger than men
1Cor. 1:25	Praise Him for His foolishness is wiser than men
Ps. 105:24	Praise Him for He has made us stronger than our enemies
1Jn. 4:4	Praise Him for He who is in us is greater than He who is in the world

Rom. 8:37	Praise Him for He has made us to be more than conquerors
Ps. 59:17	Praise Him for He is our strength
Ps. 140:7	Praise Him for He is our salvation in the day of battle
Nah. 1:7	Praise Him for He is our stronghold in the day of trouble
Ps. 18:18	Praise Him for He is our support in the day of disaster
Ps. 9:9	Praise Him for He is our refuge in times of trouble
Matt. 6:13	Praise Him when He delivers you from the evil one
Jn. 17:15	Praise Him when He keeps you from the evil one
2Thess. 3:3	Praise Him when He guards you from the evil one
Jas. 4:7	Praise Him when He gives you power to resist the evil one
Lu. 22:31-32	Praise Him when He prays for you so that you would have great faith to battle the evil one
Rom. 16:20	Praise Him when He crushes the evil one under your feet
1Jn. 2:14	Praise Him when you overcome the evil one
1Jn. 5:18	Praise Him when the evil one cannot touch you

Chapter Six

Praise Him For His
Exceptional Greatness

Great and marvelous are Your works, Lord God Almighty! Just and true are Your ways, O King of the saints!
Rev. 15:3

He Is Great

Ps. 150:2	Praise Him for His excellent greatness
Ps. 145:17	Praise Him for He is righteous and gracious in every way possible
Dt. 7:21	Praise Him for He is a great and awesome God
Dt. 32:4	Praise Him for He is true and upright
2Sam. 22:4	Praise Him for He is worthy to be praised
2Sam. 22:47	Praise Him for He is alive
1Chr. 16:27	Praise Him for honor and majesty are before Him
1Chr. 29:11	Praise Him for all the power, glory, victory and majesty belong to Him
2Chr. 20:21	Praise Him for He is beautiful in holiness (Ps. 29:2)
Ps. 40:5	Praise Him for He does wonderful things
Ps. 126:3	Praise Him for He does great things for you
Dt. 10:21	Praise Him for you see the great things He does

He Is Great And Capable In Every Way

Eph. 3:20-21 Praise Him—He is able

1Tim. 2:2 Praise Him—His life is peaceable
Rom. 12:1 Praise Him—His call is reasonable
Rom. 12:2 Praise Him—His will is acceptable
Hag. 2:7 Praise Him—His glory is desirable
2Tim. 3:16 Praise Him—His Word is profitable
Pr. 22:21 Praise Him—His words are reliable
Ps. 111:3 Praise Him—His work is honorable
Hos. 12:5 Praise Him—His name is memorable
Rom. 11:29 Praise Him—His gifts are irrevocable
Matt. 21:33 Praise Him—His wisdom is a parable
Acts 4:16 Praise Him—His miracles are notable
Matt. 3:12 Praise Him—His fire is unquenchable
1Tim. 6:16 Praise Him—His light is unapproachable
Heb. 12:22 Praise Him—His angels are innumerable
1Cor. 9:25 Praise Him—His crowns are imperishable

Ps. 102:27 Praise Him—He is immutable
2Sam. 22:31 Praise Him—He is impeccable
Is. 54:10 Praise Him—He is immovable (Jas. 1:17)
Rom. 11:33 Praise Him—He is immeasurable (Job. 9:10)
Dt. 32:4 Praise Him—He is infallible
Ex. 15:11 Praise Him—He is inimitable
Heb. 12:1-2 Praise Him—He is indubitable
Heb. 10:12-14 Praise Him—He is indispensable
Job 36:26 Praise Him—He is incomprehensible
1Pet. 2:6-7 Praise Him—He is invaluable (Ps. 36:7)
Ps. 66:3 Praise Him—He is invincible (Ps. 60:12)
Eph. 1:17-21 Praise Him—He is incredible (Acts 26:8)
2Cor. 9:14-15 Praise Him—He is indescribable (Ps. 40:5)
Ps. 89:6, 8 Praise Him—He is incomparable (Dt. 3:24)
Job 9:32-33 Praise Him—He is incontrovertible (Job 23)
1Pet. 1:23 Praise Him—He is incorruptible (Job 34:10, 12)
Heb. 12:27-28 Praise Him—He is unshakable
2Tim. 2:13 Praise Him—He is undeniable
Ps. 119:93 Praise Him—He is unforgettable
2Chr. 6:18 Praise Him—He is uncontainable

Mal. 3:6	Praise Him—He is unchangeable
Eph. 3:8	Praise Him—He is unsurpassable
Is. 40:28	Praise Him—He is unsearchable (Job 11:7)
Ps. 145:3	Praise Him—He is unexplainable (Eccl. 3:11)
1Jn. 4:4	Praise Him—He is undefeatable (Ex. 15:3-11)
Song 1:16	Praise Him—He is beautiful
Ps. 65:11	Praise Him—He is bountiful
Ps.65:9	Praise Him—He is careful (Lu. 4:10)
1Thess. 5:24	Praise Him—He is faithful
Ex. 15:11	Praise Him—He is fearful
Ps. 66:3	Praise Him—He is forceful
Jn. 15:4-5	Praise Him—He is fruitful
Ps. 46:1	Praise Him—He is helpful
Zeph. 3:17	Praise Him—He is joyful
Jer. 3:12	Praise Him—He is merciful (Ps. 118:4)
Ps. 29:11	Praise Him—He is peaceful (Is. 9:6; 26:3)
Ps. 29:4	Praise Him—He is powerful
Ps. 69:16 (NLT)	Praise Him—He is plentiful (2Cor. 9:10)
Is. 64:8	Praise Him—He is skillful
Pr. 5:21; 15:3	Praise Him—He is watchful
Is. 9:6	Praise Him—He is wonderful
Gen. 43:29	Praise Him—He is gracious (Ex. 22:27; Ps. 145:8
Ex. 15:6, 11	Praise Him—He is glorious (Dt. 28:58; 1Chr. 29:13)
Ex. 20:5	Praise Him—He is jealous (Dt. 4:24; 5:9)
Dt. 32:4	Praise Him—He is righteous (Ps. 11:7; Jer. 12:1)
1Chr. 16:9	Praise Him—He is wondrous (Ps. 145:5)
1Chr. 16:12	Praise Him—He is marvelous (Ps. 17:7; 31:21)
Is. 26:8	Praise Him—He is famous (Ps. 1135:13; Hos. 12:5)
Joel 2:18	Praise Him—He is zealous (Zech. 1:14; 8:2)
1Pet. 2:4-7	Praise Him—He is precious (Ps. 139:17; Is. 28:16)

He Is Great And Awesome

Dt. 7:21	Praise Him for He is an awesome God
	(Dt. 10:17; Ps. 47:2; Jer. 20:11; Dan. 9:4)
Gen. 28:17	Praise Him in the awesome place of His presence
Ex. 34:10	Praise Him for He does awesome things among us
	(Dt. 10:21)

Ps. 65:5	Praise Him for He does awesome deeds in righteousness
Ps. 66:3-5	Praise Him for He does awesome works that overtake the enemy
Ps. 145:6	Praise Him for He does awesome and mighty acts (Is. 28:21)
Dt. 28:58	Praise Him for He has an awesome name (Ps. 99:3; 111:9)
Job 37:22	Praise Him for He is awesome in majesty
Ps. 45:4	Praise Him for He teaches us awesome things
Song 6:4, 10	Praise Him for He has made us awesome as an army with banners
Joel 2:31	Praise Him for He is bringing a new and awesome day upon the earth (Zeph. 2:11; Acts 2:20)
Ps. 114:7	Praise Him when the earth and mountains tremble in His presence (Ps. 68:8)
Is. 41:15	Praise Him when the mountains are threshed in His presence
Ps. 97:5	Praise Him when the mountains melt like wax in His presence
Ex. 19:18	Praise Him when the mountains smoke in His presence
Mk. 11:23	Praise Him when the mountains are cast into the sea in His presence (Rev. 8:8)
Is. 49:3; 55:12	Praise Him when the mountains sing in His presence
Amos 9:13	Praise Him when the mountains drip with water, new wine and milk in His presence (Joel 3:18)
2Chr. 6:14	Praise Him for there is no god like Him
Job 36:24	Praise Him for His mighty works
Rev. 16:7	Praise Him for His judgments are true and righteous
Dt. 32:3	Praise Him and ascribe greatness to Him
Ps. 72:18	Praise Him for He only does wondrous things
Lu. 5:26	Praise Him when you see Him do wondrous things
Ps. 75:1	Praise Him for He does wondrous works that speak of Him

His Great Attributes

1Jn. 4:8	Praise Him for He is love
Ps. 117:2	Praise Him for He is kind
Ps. 48:1	Praise Him for He is great
1Chr. 16:34	Praise Him for He is good
Ps. 145:8	Praise Him for He is gracious
Ps. 145:8	Praise Him for He is slow to anger
Ps. 145:8	Praise Him for He is full of compassion
Phil. 4:8	Praise Him for He is true
Phil. 4:8	Praise Him for He is noble
Phil. 4:8	Praise Him for He is just
Phil. 4:8	Praise Him for He is pure
Phil. 4:8	Praise Him for He is lovely
Phil. 4:8	Praise Him for He is good
Phil. 4:8	Praise Him for He is virtuous
Phil. 4:8	Praise Him for He is worthy of praise
Jn. 1:14	Praise Him for His unfailing love
Ps. 16:11	Praise Him for His unceasing joy
2Cor. 3:18	Praise Him for His unveiling glory
Jude 1:3	Praise Him for His unchanging truth
Num. 14:21	Praise Him for His undying covenant
Ps. 96:9	Praise Him for His unsettling splendor
Rom. 10:21	Praise Him for His unyielding patience
Song 8:6	Praise Him for His unrelenting affection
Ps. 117:2	Praise Him for His unassuming kindness
Ps. 21:1-7	Praise Him for His unwavering blessings
Heb. 6:17-18	Praise Him for His uncompromising promises
Eph. 1:5	Praise Him for His unbending will to do us good

His Great Excellence And Glory

Job 37:23	Praise Him for He is excellent in power
Ps. 150:2	Praise Him for He is excellent in greatness
Is. 28:29	Praise Him for He is excellent in guidance

Ps. 8:9	Praise Him for His name is excellent in all the earth
Heb. 1:4	Praise Him for His name is more excellent than the angels' names
Is. 12:5	Praise Him for He has done excellent things
2Pet. 1:17	Praise Him for He speaks out of excellent glory
Ps. 16:3	Praise Him for He has made us His excellent ones
Ps. 145:5	Praise Him for He is majestic in His splendor
Ez. 16:4	Praise Him for He adorns us with His splendor
2Pet. 1:16	Praise Him for He is coming again in majestic splendor
Rev. 18:1	Praise Him for He fills the earth with His splendor
Hab. 2:14	Praise Him for He fills the earth with glory
Hag. 2:7	Praise Him for He fills His house with glory
Col. 1:27	Praise Him for He fills you with glory
Ps. 8:1	Praise Him-His glory is above the heavens
Ps. 57:11	Praise Him-His glory is above all the earth
Ps. 99:2	Praise Him-His glory is above all the peoples
Eph. 4:6	Praise Him-He is above all, and through all, and in all
Col. 1:11	Praise Him for His power is glorious
Neh. 9:5	Praise Him for His name is glorious
Ps. 66:2	Praise Him for His praise is glorious
Ps. 111:3	Praise Him for His work is glorious
Ps. 145:5	Praise Him for His majesty is glorious
Ps. 145:12	Praise Him for His kingdom is glorious
Is. 30:30	Praise Him for His voice is glorious
Is. 42:21	Praise Him for His law is glorious
Is. 60:7	Praise Him for His house (temple) is glorious
Is. 63:1	Praise Him for His clothing is glorious
Jer. 17:12	Praise Him for His throne is glorious
Lu. 13:17	Praise Him for His acts are glorious
Rom. 8:21	Praise Him for His liberty is glorious
2Cor. 3:8	Praise Him for His ministry is glorious
2Cor. 3:9-11	Praise Him for His covenants are glorious
Eph. 1:18	Praise Him for His inheritance is glorious
Eph. 5:27	Praise Him for His Church is glorious
Phil. 3:21	Praise Him for His body is glorious

1Tim. 1:11	Praise Him for His Gospel is glorious
Titus 2:13	Praise Him for His return is glorious
Jude 1:14	Praise Him for His presence is glorious
Ps. 87:3	Praise Him for the city of His presence is glorious
Is. 11:10	Praise Him for the place of His presence is glorious
Is. 60:13	Praise Him for the place of His feet is glorious
Lu. 19:37	Praise Him when you see His miracles
Lu. 23:47	Praise Him when you see His death
Lu. 24:50-53	Praise Him when you see His ascension
Rev. 1:7	Praise Him when you see His return
Ps. 97:6	Praise Him when you see His glory
	(Is. 40:5; Jn. 11:40; 17:24)
Is. 60:2	Praise Him when His glory is seen in you (Is. 62:2)
2Cor. 3:18	Praise Him when you are transformed into His image from glory to glory
2Cor. 4:6	Praise Him when His glory shines out of you
Col. 1:27	Praise Him when He is in you and there is glory
Col. 3:3	Praise Him when you are in Him and there is glory
Ex. 15:6	Praise Him for He is glorious in power
Ex. 15:11	Praise Him for He is glorious in holiness

His Great Kindness

Ps. 63:3	Praise Him when His lovingkindness is better than life
Ps. 36:7	Praise Him when His lovingkindness is precious
Ps. 69:16	Praise Him when His lovingkindness is good
Ps. 103:4	Praise Him when His lovingkindness crowns us
Ps. 17:7	Praise Him when His lovingkindness is shown to us
Ps. 26:3	Praise Him when His lovingkindness is before our eyes
Jer. 31:3	Praise Him when His lovingkindness draws us
Ps. 40:11	Praise Him when His lovingkindness preserves us
Ps. 119:88	Praise Him when His lovingkindness revives us
Ps. 144:2	Praise Him when His lovingkindness delivers us

Ps. 92:2	Praise Him when His lovingkindness is with us in the morning
Ps. 42:8	Praise Him when His lovingkindness is with us through the day
Ps. 51:1	Praise Him when His lovingkindness releases His mercy
Jer. 9:24	Praise Him when His lovingkindness is released in the earth
Jer. 32:18	Praise Him when His lovingkindness is revealed to thousands
Hos. 2:19	Praise Him when His lovingkindness is our marriage promise
Jonah 4:2	Praise Him when His lovingkindness is in abundance
Ps. 48:9	Praise Him when you meditate on His lovingkindness
Ps. 107:43	Praise Him when you understand His lovingkindness
Is. 54:10	Praise Him for His kindness will never depart from you—even when the mountains and hills depart

His Great Love And Mercy

1Ki. 10:9	Praise Him for He loves Israel forever (2Chr. 2:11)
Ps. 37:28	Praise Him for He loves justice
Ps. 11:7	Praise Him for He loves righteousness (Ps. 33:5; 146:8)
Ps. 87:2	Praise Him for He loves the gates of Zion
Pr. 3:12	Praise Him for He loves those He corrects like a father loves His son (Heb. 12:6)
Eph. 5:29	Praise Him for He loves the Church (Rom. 1:7; 5:5; 1Thess. 1:4; 1Jn. 4:16)
2Cor. 9:7	Praise Him for He loves the cheerful giver
Rom. 8:38	Praise Him for there is nothing that can take us from His love
Ps. 36:5	Praise Him when you detect His mercy and faithfulness reaching as far as the clouds
Lam. 3:22-23	Praise Him when you discover His mercy and faithfulness in the morning

Ps. 89:1	Praise Him when you declare His mercy and faithfulness to all generations (De. 7:9; Ps. 119:90)
Ps. 89:24	Praise Him when you determine His mercy and faithfulness is at your side
Heb. 2:17	Praise Him when you delight in Hs mercy and faithfulness as your personal High Priest
Micah 7:18	Praise Him for He delights in showing mercy
Ps. 98:3	Praise Him for He remembers His mercy
Rom. 9:15-18	Praise Him for He chooses to show mercy
2Cor. 1:3	Praise Him for He is the Father of every mercy
Eph. 2:4	Praise Him for He is rich in mercy
Jas. 5:11	Praise Him for He is full of mercy
Dt. 7:9	Praise Him for He keeps covenant and mercy for a thousand generations
Lu. 1:50	Praise Him for His mercy is from generation to generation
Ps. 103:17	Praise Him for His mercy is from everlasting to everlasting (Ps. 100:5; 103:17)
Ps. 89:2	Praise Him for His mercy lasts forever
Ps. 107:1	Praise Him for His mercy endures forever (Ps. 136)
Pr. 28:13	Praise Him for His mercy is for those who confess and forsake their sin
Lu. 1:50	Praise Him for His mercy is for those who fear Him
Is. 14:1	Praise Him for His mercy is for the descendants of Jacob
Hos. 2:19, 23	Praise Him for His mercy is the mark of His marriage covenant with us
Hos. 10:12	Praise Him for His mercy is our reward for righteousness
Matt. 5:7	Praise Him for His mercy is for all who show mercy
Zech. 7:9	Praise Him for His mercy proceeds from justice (Ps. 89:14; Is. 16:5; Hos. 2:19; 12:6; Micah. 6:8; Matt. 23:23)
Jas. 2:13	Praise Him for His mercy triumphs over judgment
Jas. 3:17	Praise Him for His mercy fills all heavenly wisdom
Is. 16:5	Praise Him for His mercy establishes His throne

Heb. 4:16	Praise Him for His mercy is found at His throne
Is. 63:7-9	Praise Him for His mercy is full of compassion and redemption
Ps. 119:58	Praise Him for His mercy is in His Word
Num. 14:18	Praise Him for His mercy is abundant (Ps. 86:5; 1Pet. 1:3)
Ps. 69:16	Praise Him for His mercy is tender (Ps. 25:6; 40:11)
Ps. 103:11	Praise Him for His mercy is great
Ps. 86:13	Praise Him for His mercy is very great
Rom. 12:8	Praise Him for His mercy is joyous
Ps. 69:16	Praise Him for His mercy is plentiful
Ps. 13:5	Praise Him for His mercy is trustworthy (Ps. 52:8)
Ps. 31:7	Praise Him for His mercy is praiseworthy (Rom. 15:9)
Ps. 36:5	Praise Him for His mercy is as vast as the heavens
Ps. 108:4	Praise Him for His mercy is higher than the heavens
Ps. 85:10	Praise Him for His mercy is joined to truth
Ps. 89:14	Praise Him for His mercy is before His face
Pr. 3:3	Praise Him for His mercy is bound around our necks
Pr. 3:3	Praise Him for His mercy is written on our hearts
Gal. 6:16	Praise Him for His mercy is upon us
Jude 1:2	Praise Him for His mercy is multiplied upon us
Ps. 119:64	Praise Him for His mercy is filling the earth
1Tim. 1:2	Praise Him for His mercy greets us (2Tim. 1:2)
Ps. 25:10	Praise Him for His mercy leads us
Pr. 14:22	Praise Him for His mercy leads us to do good
Pr. 21:21	Praise Him for His mercy leads us to life
Pr. 21:21	Praise Him for His mercy leads us to righteousness
Pr. 21:21	Praise Him for His mercy leads us to honor
Is. 49:10	Praise Him for His mercy leads us to springs of water
Ps. 23:6	Praise Him for His mercy follows us
Ps. 32:10	Praise Him for His mercy surrounds us
Ps. 109:26	Praise Him for His mercy saves us (Tit. 3:5)
Ps. 109:21	Praise Him for His mercy delivers us
Pr. 20:28	Praise Him for His mercy protects us
Ps. 89:24	Praise Him for His mercy abides with us
Ps. 89:28	Praise Him for His mercy keeps us
Ps. 90:14	Praise Him for His mercy satisfies us
Ps. 94:18	Praise Him for His mercy holds us up
Ps. 119:159	Praise Him for His mercy revives us

Ps. 119:76	Praise Him for His mercy comforts us
Ps. 103:4	Praise Him for His mercy crowns us
Col. 3:12	Praise Him for His mercy clothes us
Pr. 16:6	Praise Him for His mercy covers us
2Cor. 1:3	Praise Him for His mercy encourages us
Lu. 1:78	Praise Him for His mercy brings us light
Jude 1:21	Praise Him as you keep looking for His mercy that leads to eternal life (Rom. 6:23)
Ps. 101:1	Praise Him for His mercy has become our song
Ps. 59:16	Praise Him for His mercy is our song in the morning

His Greatness Goes Wherever He Goes

Dt. 33:26	Praise Him for He rides on the heavens
Ps. 68:4	Praise Him for He rides on the clouds
Ps. 104:3	Praise Him for He rides on the wind
Micah 6:8	Praise Him when He walks with you
Matt. 14:25	Praise Him when He walks on water
Dan. 3:25	Praise Him when He walks in the fire
Lev. 26:12	Praise Him when He walks among you
Ps. 104:3	Praise Him when He walks on the wind
Gen. 3:8	Praise Him when He walks in the garden
Hab. 3:15	Praise Him when He walks through the sea
Song 2:8	Praise Him when He walks on the mountains
Job 22:14	Praise Him when He walks above the heavens
Ex 33:22	Praise Him for He processed before Moses and spoke His name (Ex. 34:5-7)
Ps. 68:7	Praise Him for He processed through the wilderness
Ps. 68:24	Praise Him for He processed in the sanctuary
Matt. 21:1-11	Praise Him for He processed into Jerusalem
2Cor. 2:14	Praise Him for He leads us in triumphant procession
Ps. 132:8	Praise Him—He arises upon the Ark of His presence
Ps. 3:7	Praise Him—He arises to save us (Ps. 7:6)
Ps. 9:19	Praise Him—He arises to judge the nations (Ps. 82:8)
Ps. 10:12	Praise Him—He arises to lift His hand to help us

Ps. 68:1	Praise Him—He arises to scatter His enemies
Ps. 102:13	Praise Him—He arises with mercy for Zion
Is. 60:1-2	Praise Him—He arises upon us with glory
Mal. 4:2	Praise Him—He arises with healing in His wings

Zech. 2:10-11	Praise Him for He dwells in our midst
Ps. 145:18	Praise Him for He is near (Eph. 2:13; Jas. 4:8)
Rev. 21:3	Praise Him for He tabernacles and dwells with us

His Greatness Endures Forever

1Chr. 16:34	Praise Him for His mercy endures forever
Ps. 111:3	Praise Him for His righteousness endures forever
Ps. 111:10	Praise Him for His praise endures forever
Ps. 117:2	Praise Him for His truth endures forever
Ps. 119:160	Praise Him for His righteous judgments endure forever
Ps. 135:13	Praise Him for His name endures forever
1Pet. 1:25	Praise Him for His Word endures forever

His Greatness Is Without Equal

1Cor. 13:10	Praise Him for He is perfect
Rom. 12:2	Praise Him for His will is perfect
Ps. 19:7	Praise Him for His law is perfect
1Jn. 4:18	Praise Him for His love is perfect
Dt. 32:4	Praise Him for His work is perfect
Is. 26:3	Praise Him for His peace is perfect
Jas. 1:17	Praise Him for His gifts are perfect
2Sam. 22:31	Praise Him for His ways are perfect
Job 36:4	Praise Him for His knowledge is perfect (Job 37:16)
2Cor. 12:9	Praise Him for His strength is perfect when we are weak
Matt. 21:16	Praise Him for His praise is perfect through the lips of children

Dt. 32:4	Praise Him for He is without injustice
Job 5:8-9	Praise Him for He does marvelous things without number
Jn. 1:3	Praise Him for nothing was made without Him

Jn. 15:5	Praise Him for nothing can be done without Him
Eph. 1:4	Praise Him for He chose us to be before Him without blame (Eph. 5:27; 2Pet. 3:14; Rev. 14:5)
Heb. 4:15	Praise Him for He is without sin
1Pet. 1:19	Praise Him for He is a spotless Lamb without blemish
2Cor. 9:15	Praise Him for the indescribable gift of Christ
Eph. 1:3	Praise Him for blessing us with every spiritual blessing because of Christ (Eph. 5:20)
Eph. 1:6	Praise Him for the glory of the grace of Christ

He Is Greater Than All

Phil. 2:9	Praise Him for His name is above all names
Ps. 95:3	Praise Him for He is a God above all gods
Rev. 19:6	Praise Him for He is the King of all kings
1Tim. 6:15	Praise Him for He is Lord of Lords
Ps. 63:3	Praise Him for His kindness is better than life
Ps. 84:10	Praise Him for a day in His courts is better than a thousand elsewhere
Pr. 8:19	Praise Him for His wisdom is better than gold
Song 1:2	Praise Him for His love is better than wine
Heb 1:4	Praise Him for He is better than the angels
Jn. 15:13	Praise Him for His love is greater than any other
Ps. 109:103	Praise Him for His words are sweeter than honey
Job 23:12	Praise Him for His words are to be treasured more than food
Ps. 40:5	Praise Him for His thoughts of us are more than can be numbered
Ps. 119:127	Praise Him for His commandments are to be loved more than fine gold
Song 1:4	Praise Him for we remember His love more than wine
Is. 52:14	Praise Him for His face was marred more than any man
Heb. 1:9	Praise Him for He has anointed us with joy more than any others

His Greatness Is Lavished On Us

1Pet. 5:7	Praise Him when you are comforted by His care
Ps. 86:15	Praise Him when you are changed by His compassion
Titus 3:1-8	Praise Him when you are governed by His grace
Lu. 17:15	Praise Him when you are humbled by His healing (Matt. 9:8; 15:31; Lu. 18:43; 19:37)
Ps. 119:7	Praise Him when you are jeweled by His judgments
Ps. 146:7	Praise Him when you are justified by His justice
1Tim. 6:16	Praise Him when you are loved by His light
Song 1:4	Praise Him when you are loosed by His love
Ps. 107:1	Praise Him when you are mastered by His mercy
Job 37:23	Praise Him when you are propelled by His power
Ps. 95:2	Praise Him when you are preserved by His presence
Job 19:25-27	Praise Him when you are reformed by His redemption
Jer. 16:19	Praise Him when you are restored by His refuge
Eph. 3:8	Praise Him when you are rewarded by His riches
Dan. 2:19-23, 47	Praise Him when you are strengthened by His secrets
Zeph. 3:16	Praise Him when you are soothed by His song
Ps. 119:171	Praise Him when you are secured by His statutes
Ps. 25:5	Praise Him when you are taught by His truth
2Tim. 3:16-17	Praise Him when you are wakened by His Word
Ps. 37:3	Praise Him when you are fed by His faithfulness
Ps. 18:35	Praise Him when you are graced by His gentleness
Ps. 107:8, 15	Praise Him when you are guided by His goodness
Ps 31:21	Praise Him when you are kindled by His kindness
Ps. 63:3	Praise Him when you are lavished with His lovingkindness
Is. 54:7	Praise Him when you are touched by His tenderness

He Wants Us To Know His Greatness

Ps. 76:1	Praise Him for He is known in praise (Judah)
Matt. 11:27	Praise Him when He reveals knowledge of the Father to you
Dan. 11:32	Praise Him when you know Him for those who know Him will do great things
Hos. 6:3	Praise Him when you run after knowing Him

Hos. 2:20	Praise Him when you know Him and are betrothed to Him
Is. 45:3	Praise Him when you know that He is God
Deut 4:35	Praise Him when you know that He is God alone
Is. 60:16	Praise Him when you know that He is Savior and Redeemer
Is. 45:6	Praise Him when you know from the rising of the sun until it sets that He is Lord and there is none beside Him
Ps. 135:5	Praise Him when you know that the Lord is great and is above all gods
Ps. 83:18	Praise Him when you know that the Lord is high above all the earth
Is. 58:2	Praise Him when you delight to know His ways
Dan. 11:32	Praise Him when you know Him and do exploits
Ps. 100:3	Praise Him when you know that the Lord is God and He made you—the sheep of His pasture
Jn. 10:3-4, 27	Praise Him when you know His voice because you are His sheep
Ez. 34:30	Praise Him when you know that He is with you and that you are His people
Dt. 7:9	Praise Him when you know that He is faithful
Ps. 119:75	Praise Him when you know that His judgments are right and fair
Job 19:25	Praise Him when you know that your Redeemer lives
Job 19:26	Praise Him when you know that in your flesh you will see God
Ps. 51:6	Praise Him when you know wisdom (Eccl. 7:25)
Eccl. 3:14	Praise Him when you know that whatever God does, it shall endure forever
Jonah 4:2	Praise Him when you know that He is gracious and merciful, slow to anger and abundant in lovingkindness (Nahum 1:3)
Matt. 9:6	Praise Him when you know that He has power to forgive sins
Rom. 8:28	Praise Him when you know that all things work together for good to those who love Him and are called according to His purpose

1Cor. 3:16	Praise Him when you know that you are the temple of God
Eph. 1:18	Praise Him when you know the hope of His calling and the riches of His glory
Phil. 3:10	Praise Him when you know the power of His resurrection
Phil. 3:10	Praise Him when you know the fellowship of His suffering
2Pet. 1:3	Praise Him when you know Him more and more
1Jn. 2:3-5	Praise Him when you know that you know Him because you obey Him
1Jn. 3:2	Praise Him when you know that when He comes, you will be like Him
1Jn. 5:15	Praise Him when you know that He hears you

Chapter Seven

Praise Him For His Perfect Work In Us

Then He who sat on the throne said,
"Behold, I make all things new." And He said to me,
"Write, for these words are true and faithful."
And He said to me, "It is done! I am the Alpha and the Omega,
the Beginning and the End.
I will give of the fountain of the water of life
freely to him who thirsts.
"He who overcomes shall inherit all things,
and I will be his God and he shall be My son.
Rev. 21:5-7

He Is Perfect In All Things

Eph. 5:20	Praise Him for all things
Eph. 3:9	Praise Him when He creates all things (Col. 1:16; Rev. 4:11)
Is. 44:24	Praise Him when He makes all things (Jer. 10:16; 51:19; Jn. 1:3)
2Cor. 5:17	Praise Him when He makes all things new
Eph. 1:22	Praise Him when He puts all things under His feet (Ps. 8:6)
Ps. 57:2	Praise Him when He does all things for you
Rom. 8:32	Praise Him when He freely gives you all things
Matt. 19:26	Praise Him when He makes all things possible (Mk. 9:23; 10:27)
Jn. 14:26	Praise Him when He teaches you all things (1Jn. 2:27)
Acts 13:39	Praise Him when He justifies you from all things
Rom. 8:28	Praise Him when He causes all things to work together for good

1Cor. 2:10	Praise Him when He searches all things - the deep things of God
1Cor. 1:15	Praise Him when He judges all things (Rev. 14:7)
Phil. 3:21	Praise Him when He conquers all things
Phil. 4:13	Praise Him when He strengthens us to do all things
Col. 1:20	Praise Him when He reconciles all things to Himself
1Tim. 6:6	Praise Him when He gives us richly all things to enjoy
Heb. 1:3	Praise Him when He upholds all things by His powerful Word
1Pet. 4:11	Praise Him when He is glorified through all the things we do in His name
2Pet. 1:3	Praise Him when He gives you all things to live a godly life
1Jn. 3:20	Praise Him when He knows all things
3Jn. 1:2	Praise Him when He prospers you in all things and gives you health
Rev. 21:7	Praise Him when you inherit all things

He Has A Perfect Plan For Our Salvation

Lu. 23:47	Praise Him when you recognize the Savior's death
Matt. 28:6-10	Praise Him when you recognize the risen Savior
Ps. 118:14	Praise Him when He becomes your salvation
Jer. 1:5	Praise Him for He knew us before we were formed in the womb
Eph. 1:4	Praise Him for He chose us before the world was made
2Tim. 1:9	Praise Him for He called us before the world began
Is. 53:5	Praise Him for He was wounded for our transgressions
Is. 53:5	Praise Him for He was bruised for our iniquities (sins)
Is. 53:5	Praise Him for the punishment that brought us peace was placed upon Him
Is. 53:5	Praise Him for He was whipped so that we could be healed

Gal. 2:20	Praise Him for we are crucified with Christ
Col. 2:20	Praise Him for we are dead with Christ
Rom. 6:4	Praise Him for we are buried with Christ
Eph. 2:5	Praise Him for we are made alive with Christ
Rom. 8:17	Praise Him for we are sufferers together with Christ
Col. 3:1	Praise Him for we are raised together with Christ
Rom. 8:17	Praise Him for we are glorified together with Christ
Ps. 1:3	Praise Him when you are a tree planted by rivers of water
Is. 61:3	Praise Him when you are a tree of righteousness
Jn. 15:2, 5	Praise Him when you abide in Him and bear much fruit
1Jn. 4:12-14	Praise Him when He abides in you
2Jn. 1:9	Praise Him when you abide in Him

He Has Given Us His Perfect Word

Ps. 56:4, 10	Praise His Word
1Pet. 2:2	Praise Him for His Word is milk that feeds us
Ps. 19:7-10	Praise Him for His Word is honey that is sweet
Matt. 4:4	Praise Him for His Word is bread that nourishes us
Eph. 5:26	Praise Him for His Word is water that cleanses us
Rev. 11:1-2	Praise Him for His Word is a rod that measures us
Ps. 119:105	Praise Him for His Word is a lamp that shows us the way
Jer. 23:29	Praise Him for His Word is a fire that purifies us
Jer. 23:29	Praise Him for His Word is a hammer that breaks bondages
Eph. 6:17	Praise Him for His Word is a sword that defends us
Jas. 1:21-25	Praise Him for His Word is a mirror that helps us to see ourselves correctly
1Pet. 1:23	Praise Him for His Word is a seed that produces faith and growth
Ps. 138:2	Praise Him for His Word is magnified
Ps. 119:162	Praise Him for His Word is a great treasure
2Pet. 3:5	Praise Him for His Word created all things (Gen. 1)
Ps. 33:6	Praise Him for His Word made the heavens

Ps. 119:89	Praise Him for His Word is settled in heaven
Lu. 4:32	Praise Him for His Word is filled with authority
Lu. 5:5	Praise Him for His Word creates miracles
1Ki. 8:56	Praise Him for His Word never fails
Lam. 2:17	Praise Him for His Word is fulfilled
Ps. 18:30	Praise Him for His Word is proven and true
Ps. 119:160	Praise Him for His Word is truth (Jn. 17:17)
Pa. 119:160	Praise Him for His Word endures forever
Ps. 147:15	Praise Him for His Word is swift (2Thess. 3:1)
Heb. 4:12	Praise Him for His Word is sharper than any sword
Ps. 147:18	Praise Him for His Word melts the frost and hail
Zech. 4:6	Praise Him for His Word declares the overwhelming power of the Holy Spirit
Dt. 30:14	Praise Him for His Word is very near us
Ps. 119:11	Praise Him for His Word is hidden in our hearts
Jer. 31:33	Praise Him for His Word is written on our hearts
Jer. 15:16	Praise Him for His Word is the joy of our hearts
Ps. 130:5	Praise Him for His Word contains hope (Ps. 119:114)
Ps. 119:50	Praise Him for His Word comforts and gives us life
1Jn. 2:14	Praise Him for His Word abides in us
Ps. 107:20	Praise Him for His Word heals and delivers us
Ps. 119:28	Praise Him for His Word strengthens us
Ps. 119:41	Praise Him for His Word saves us
Ps. 119:107	Praise Him for His Word revives us
Eph. 5:26	Praise Him for His Word washes us
1Tim. 4:5	Praise Him for His Word sanctifies us
Pr. 16:20	Praise Him for His Word prospers us
1Pet. 2:2	Praise Him for His Word feeds us
Job. 23:12	Praise Him for His Word is better than food
Ps. 119:140	Praise Him for His Word is very pure
Ps. 119:9	Praise Him for His Word keeps us pure
1Jn. 2:5	Praise Him for His Word causes His love to be perfected in us
Ps. 119:169	Praise Him for His Word gives us understanding
Ps. 119:130	Praise Him for His Word gives us light
Ps. 119:133	Praise Him for His Word directs our steps
Col. 3:16	Praise Him for His Word dwells in us richly and wisely
Col. 3:16	Praise Him for His Word produces psalms, hymns and spiritual songs
Ps. 119:172	Praise Him for His Word inspires poetry and song

Is. 2:3	Praise Him for His Word comes out of Zion (people of praise)
Ps. 68:11	Praise Him for His Word is proclaimed by throngs of women
1Thess. 1:8	Praise Him for His Word goes out to everyone and every place from us
2Thess. 3:1	Praise Him for His Word spreads rapidly and brings God's glory wherever it goes
Is. 40:8	Praise Him for His Word stands forever (1Pet. 1:25)
Ps. 19:7	Praise Him for His Word is perfect, it converts the soul
Ps. 19:7	Praise Him for His Word is sure, it makes the simple wise
Ps. 19:8	Praise Him for His Word is right, it brings joy to the heart (Ps. 33:4)
Ps. 19:8	Praise Him for His Word is pure, it gives light to the eyes
Ps. 19:9	Praise Him for His Word is completely true and righteous
Ps. 19:10	Praise Him for His Word is desirable, more so than gold
Ps. 19:11	Praise Him for His Word carries a reward

He Offers Us His Perfect Help

Ps. 121:1-2	Praise Him for He helps us
Ps. 121:3	Praise Him for He steadies us
Ps. 121:4	Praise Him for He watches us
Ps. 121:5-6	Praise Him for He keeps us
Ps. 121:5	Praise Him for He shades us
Ps. 121:7	Praise Him for He preserves us
Ps. 121:8	Praise Him for He protects us
Is. 41:10	Praise Him for He is with us
Is. 41:10	Praise Him for He is our God
Is. 41:10	Praise Him for He will strengthen us
Is. 41:10	Praise Him for He will help us
Is. 41:10	Praise Him for He will hold us up

Ps. 84:3	Praise Him for He cares for every sparrow (Matt. 10:29; Lu. 12:6-7)
Matt. 6:28-30	Praise Him for He clothes every one of the lilies
Is. 59:1	Praise Him for His hand is not too short to save us
Is. 59:1	Praise Him for His ear is not too deaf to hear us

He Forms His Perfection In Us

Ps. 138:8	Praise Him—He will perfect all that concerns us
2Sam. 22:33	Praise Him—He makes our ways perfect
Matt. 5:48	Praise Him—He will make us perfect, as He is perfect
Heb. 12:23	Praise Him—He will make us just and perfect (1 Pet. 5:10)
Ez. 16:14	Praise Him—He gives us beauty that is perfect
Jas. 1:4	Praise Him—His patience is perfect and makes us perfect
Col. 4:12	Praise Him—He will help us to stand perfect and complete in all the will of God
Col. 1:28	Praise Him—He will present us as perfect in Christ (Eph. 5:27)
2Sam. 22:31	Praise Him—His way is perfect
2Sam. 22:33	Praise Him—He makes your way perfect

He Calls Us To A Perfect Faith

Matt. 15:28	Praise Him when you have great faith
Rom. 5:1	Praise Him when you are justified by faith
Acts 6:5, 8	Praise Him when you are full of faith
Rom. 4:20	Praise Him when you are strengthened in faith
Mk. 5:34	Praise Him when your faith makes you well/whole
Mk. 11:22	Praise Him when your faith is in God
Lu. 17:6	Praise Him when your faith produces miracles
1Tim. 6:12	Praise Him when you fight the fight of faith
1Pet. 1:7	Praise Him when your faith is tested (Heb. 11:17; Jas. 1:3)
2Pet. 1:5-8	Praise Him when your faith is built up
1Cor. 13:13	Praise Him when you abide in faith
Heb. 12:2	Praise Him when He finishes/completes your faith

He Has Perfect Love For Us

Ps. 139:14	Praise Him when He creates you
Num. 16:5	Praise Him when He chooses you (Ps. 65:4)
Gal. 1:15-16	Praise Him when He calls you (1Thess. 2:12; 1Pet. 2:9)
Zeph. 3:14-15	Praise Him when He clears you (2Cor. 7:11)
Ps. 51:10	Praise Him when He cleans you (Mk. 1:40-45)
Ps. 31:7	Praise Him when He considers you (Ps. 41:1)
Ps. 91:4	Praise Him when He covers you
Is. 12:1-2	Praise Him when He comforts you
Zeph. 3:17	Praise Him when He calms you
Is. 25:1	Praise Him when He counsels you
Ps. 32:8	Praise Him when He coaches you
Heb. 12:6-7	Praise Him when He chastens you
Pr. 3:12	Praise Him when He corrects you
Is. 40:11	Praise Him when He carries you
Is. 58:8	Praise Him when He cures you
Son 1:2	Praise Him when He caresses you
Is. 49:15-16	Praise Him when He cherishes you
2Cor. 3:18	Praise Him when He changes you
1Thess. 5:23	Praise Him when He comes for you
Jas. 1:12	Praise Him when He crowns you
Ps. 139:14	Praise Him when He designs you
Ps. 45:11	Praise Him when He desires you
2Sam. 22:20	Praise Him when He delights in you
Ps. 59:17	Praise Him when He defends you
Ps. 18:19	Praise Him when He delivers you
Jer. 29:11	Praise Him when He defines you
Jn. 15:8	Praise Him when He disciples you
Heb. 12:6-11	Praise Him when He disciplines you
1Cor. 3:16	Praise Him when He dwells in you

Rom. 8:15	Praise Him when He adopts us as a father
Is. 66:8-13	Praise Him when He comforts us like a mother
Pr. 18:24	Praise Him when He is a friend who is closer than a brother
Ex. 33:11	Praise Him when He is face to face like a friend
Song. 5:1	Praise Him when He loves us like a bridegroom (Matt. 25:1-12)

Jer. 31:3	Praise Him for His love is endless
1Jn. 3:1	Praise Him for His love makes us His children
1Jn. 4:16	Praise Him for His love is absolute
1Jn. 4:10	Praise Him for His love is revealed in His death
Jn. 17:26	Praise Him for His love is revealed through Jesus
Jn. 17:23	Praise Him for He loves us just as He loves Jesus
Rom. 8:38-39	Praise Him for His love will never be taken from us

He Gives Us Perfect Gifts

Dt. 26:10-11	Praise Him when you give to the Lord
Ps. 37:4	Praise Him when He gives to you

Gal. 5:22-23	Praise Him when He gives you the fruit of the Spirit
1Cor. 12:8-11	Praise Him when He gives you the gifts of the Spirit
Acts 11:15-18	Praise Him when you watch Him pour out His gifts on His people
Acts 13:46-48	Praise Him when His Gospel is preached in the earth through His people

Eph. 4:11-13	Praise Him for He gives us apostles to perfect us
Eph. 4:11-13	Praise Him for He gives us prophets to perfect us
Eph. 4:11-13	Praise Him for He gives us evangelists to perfect us
Eph. 4:11-13	Praise Him for He gives us pastors to perfect us
Eph. 4:11-13	Praise Him for He gives us teachers to perfect us

Ps. 37:30	Praise Him when He gives you the tongue of justice
Ps. 35:28	Praise Him when He gives you the tongue of righteousness and praise
Pr. 31:26	Praise Him when He gives you the tongue of kindness
Is. 50:4	Praise Him when He gives you the tongue of wisdom

Pr. 12:18	Praise Him when He gives you the tongue of the wise that brings healing
Pr. 25:15	Praise Him when He gives you the tongue of gentleness
Ps. 45:1	Praise Him when He gives you a tongue that is like the pen of skillful writer or poet
Ps. 51:14	Praise Him when He gives you a tongue that sings of His righteousness
Ps. 126:2	Praise Him when He gives you a tongue filled with singing
Ps. 119:172	Praise Him when He gives you a tongue that speaks of His Word
Pr. 10:20	Praise Him when He gives you a tongue that is like the best silver
Jas. 1:26	Praise Him when He gives you a bridled tongue

He Gives Us His Perfect Power

Ps. 68:35	Praise Him when He gives you power (Is. 40:29)
Matt. 10:1	Praise Him when He gives you power over demons and all sickness
Jas. 4:7	Praise Him when He gives you power to resist the devil and watch him flee from you
Lu. 5:24	Praise Him that He has power to forgive sin (Is. 1:18)
Acts 1:8	Praise Him when the power of the Holy Spirit comes on you
Acts 6:8	Praise Him when you are full of faith and power to perform wonders and miracles
Eph. 6:10	Praise Him when you are strong with the Lord's mighty power
Phil. 3:10	Praise Him when you know the power of His resurrection
2Tim. 1:7	Praise Him when He gives you a spirit of power over fear

Ps. 106:47	Praise Him when He causes you to triumph in praise
Ps. 149:6	Praise Him when He places the sword of praise in your mouth and hand
2Sam. 22:34	Praise Him when He makes your feet like a deer
2Sam. 22:35	Praise Him when He trains your hands for war (Ex. 17:9-12; Ps. 18:34)
Ps. 144:1	Praise Him when He trains your fingers for battle

Chapter Eight

Praise Him For His Precious Promises

These things says the First and the Last,
who was dead, and came to life
Rev. 2:8

His Covenant Promises

Gen. 1:26-30	Praise Him for His covenant promise to Adam (Gen. 3:14-19)
Gen. 9:1-17	Praise Him for His covenant promise to Noah (Gen. 6:17-22)
Gen. 12:1-3, 7	Praise Him for His covenant promise to Abraham (Gen. 13:14-17; 15:4-21; 17:4-16; 22:15-18)
Ex. 19:4—24:8	Praise Him for His covenant promise to Moses (Dt. 29-30)
Num. 25:1-13	Praise Him for His covenant promise to the Levites (Neh. 13:29-31; Jer. 44:20-22; Mal. 2:4-10)
2Sam. 7:10-16	Praise Him for His covenant promise to David (2 Samuel 7:10-16; 1Chr. 17:7-15; Ps. 89:33-37)
Heb. 8:1-10:39	Praise Him for His covenant promise to the Church—this is the New Covenant (Jer. 31:31-34; Rom. 10:4; Gal. 3:13-20; Heb. 7:7, 22; 8:6; 9:23; 10:10, 24; 12:24)

The Truth Concerning His Covenants And Promises

Neh. 1:5	Praise Him for He is a covenant keeping God (Dt. 7:9)
Ps. 25:10	Praise Him for He gives mercy and truth to all who keep His covenant (Ps. 103:17-18)

Ez. 16:60	Praise Him for His covenant is everlasting and He remembers every detail of it
Is. 49:8	Praise Him for He has made us His covenant people (Is. 42:6)
Matt. 26:28	Praise Him for He has shed His own blood so that we might have a new and better covenant (Heb. 8:6-13)
Ez. 16:8	Praise Him for all of His covenants are an expression of His love and grace
Gal. 3:14	Praise Him—the promise He gave to Abraham is also for the Gentiles
Heb. 6:13	Praise Him—when He gave His promise to Abraham He swore by Himself
Heb. 8:6	Praise Him—the covenant promise He gave to us is made up of even better promises than those He gave to Abraham
Gal. 4:28	Praise Him—we are the children of promise
Heb. 8:6	Praise Him—He is the Mediator of His promises (Heb. 9:15)
2Cor. 7:1	Praise Him—His promises lead us to perfect holiness
2Pet. 1:4	Praise Him—He has given us rich and precious promises

He Is Faithful To Keep All His Promises

Num. 23:19	Praise Him for He is not a man who lies—He will do what He has promised (Rom. 4:21; Heb. 6:18)
2Pet. 3:9	Praise Him for He is not slack (or slow) concerning His promises
Ps. 89:34	Praise Him for He will not break His promises or anything that has gone out of His lips
Heb. 10:23	Praise Him for He is faithful to all His promises
1Ki. 8:56	Praise Him for He keeps His promises even when we are unfaithful (1Ki. 8:56)
Dt. 7:9	Praise Him for He keeps His promises for a thousand generations (Ps. 105:8)
Is. 46:11	Praise Him for He will bring all His promises to pass
Titus 1:2	Praise Him for His promises to us were established before the world began
1Chr. 17:23	Praise Him for His promises last forever

| 2Cor. 1:20 | Praise Him for all His promises are fulfilled in and through Jesus |
| Eph. 1:13-14 | Praise Him for we are sealed with the Holy Spirit of promise—our guarantee that He will do what He has promised |

His Promises To Us

Heb. 13:5	Praise Him for He promises He will never leave us
Josh. 1:5	Praise Him for He promises He will never forsake us
Matt. 28:20	Praise Him for He promises to be with us always
1Jn. 4:10, 16, 19	Praise Him for He promises to love us
1Cor. 8:3	Praise Him for He promises to know us
2Cor. 6:16	Praise Him for He promises to be our God
Is. 41:10	Praise Him for He promises to be with us
Ps. 4:3	Praise Him for He promises to hear us when we pray
Ps. 145:18	Praise Him for He promises to be near us when we call
Dt. 4:29	Praise Him for He promises to let us find Him
Joel 2:32	Praise Him for He promises to deliver us
Jer. 33:3	Praise Him for He promises to answer us
Phil. 4:19	Praise Him for He promises to supply all our needs
Is. 40:11	Praise Him for He promises to feed us
Dt. 11:13-14	Praise Him for He promises to give us rain
Dt. 28:12	Praise Him for He promises to prosper us (Ps. 1:3)
Ps. 5:12	Praise Him for He promises to bless us with favor
Ps. 84:11	Praise Him for He promises to be our sun and shield
Ps. 84:11	Praise Him for He promises to give us all good things
Is. 32:18	Praise Him for He promises to give us peace
Heb. 4:1	Praise Him for He promises to give us rest
Jas. 1:5	Praise Him for He promises to give us wisdom
Gal. 3:14	Praise Him for He promises to give us the Holy Spirit
Ps. 34:7	Praise Him for He promises to give us angels
Ps. 37:4	Praise Him for He promises to give us the desires of our heart
Ez. 36:26	Praise Him for He promises to give us a new heart
Ez. 36:26	Praise Him for He promises to give us a new spirit
Ps. 103:3	Praise Him for He promises to forgive all our sins
1Jn. 1:9	Praise Him for He promises to cleanse us from all sin
Hos. 14:4	Praise Him for He promises to restore our backsliding

Dt. 7:15	Praise Him for He promises to take away all sickness
Ps. 103:3	Praise Him for He promises to heal all our diseases
Acts 16:31	Praise Him for He promises to save our family
Ps. 115:14	Praise Him for He promises to bless our children
Ez. 34:25, 28	Praise Him for He promises to protect us
Ps. 145:20	Praise Him for He promises to preserve us
Ps. 32:6-7	Praise Him for He promises to keep us from trouble
Ps. 27:14	Praise Him for He promises to strengthen us
1Pet. 5:7	Praise Him for He promises to care for us
Ps. 46:11	Praise Him for He promises to become our refuge
Ps. 125:2	Praise Him for He promises to surround us
Dt. 33:27	Praise Him for He promises to hold us with His arms
Phil. 4:13	Praise Him for He promises to help us do all things
1Jn. 5:4-5	Praise Him for He promises to help us overcome sin
Is. 59:19	Praise Him for He promises to vanquish our enemies
Dt. 28:7	Praise Him for He promises to make our enemies who come against us one way, run from us seven ways
Dt. 20:4	Praise Him for He promises to fight for us
Is. 41:11-12	Praise Him for He promises to shame all who fight us
Ps. 138:8	Praise Him for He promises to perfect everything that concerns us
Rom. 8:28	Praise Him for He promises to work all things out for good
2Cor. 4:16-17	Praise Him for He promises to renew us day by day
Ps. 119:105	Praise Him for He promises to light our way
Ps. 37:23	Praise Him for He promises to order our steps
Pr. 3:6	Praise Him for He promises to direct our paths
Ps. 48:14	Praise Him for He promises to guide us through life
Is. 58:11	Praise Him for He promises to guide us continually
Jn. 16:13	Praise Him for He promises to guide us into all truth
Ps. 48:14	Praise Him for He promises to guide us to our death
Phil. 1:6	Praise Him for He promises to complete His work in us
1Thess. 5:23	Praise Him for He promises to entirely sanctify us
Jude 24	Praise Him for He promises to keep us from falling
Jude 24	Praise Him for He promises to present us as faultless
Ex. 19:5	Praise Him for He promises to make us His treasure
Ps. 91:14-15	Praise Him for He promises to honor us (1Sam. 2:30)
Zeph. 3:17	Praise Him for He promises to rejoice over us

Jas. 2:5	Praise Him for He promises to give us the kingdom
1Jn. 5:12	Praise Him for He promises to give us life
Jn. 10:10	Praise Him for He promises to give us abundant life
Dt. 5:33	Praise Him for He promises to give us long life
1Jn. 2:25	Praise Him for He promises to give us eternal life
Jn. 3:16; 6:47	Praise Him for He promises to give us everlasting life
Jn. 14:3	Praise Him for He promises to return for us
Matt. 24:30	Praise Him for He promises to appear in power and great glory
Col. 3:4	Praise Him for He promises to have us appear with Him in glory
1Jn. 3:2	Praise Him for He promises to make us like Him when He appears, for we will see Him as He is
Rom. 8:11	Praise Him for He promises to raise us up from death (Jn. 11:25-26; 2Cor. 4:14)
Rev. 22:12, 20	Praise Him for He promises to reward every man according to His works (Matt. 16:27)
Jn. 14:2-3	Praise Him for He promises to prepare a place for us to be with Him forever (1Thess. 4:16-17)
1Jn. 2:17	Praise Him for He promises to have us live with Him forever (Jn. 6:47)
Jas. 1:12	Praise Him for He promises to crown us with life
2Pet. 3:13	Praise Him for He promises to give us a new heaven and a new earth
Jer. 31, 33, 50	Praise Him for He promises to love and bless Israel forever (Joel 3; Amos 9:14-15; Zech. 10; Rom. 11)
Gen. 12:3	Praise Him for He promises to bless those who bless Israel
Gen. 12:3	Praise Him for He promises to bless all the earth through Israel
Ez. 39:27	Praise Him for He promises to reveal His holiness to the nations through Israel's restoration
Heb. 6:12	Praise Him for we inherit all these promises through faith and patience

Chapter Nine

Praise Him For His Gracious Kindness
He Causes Us To Overcome
Through Every Circumstance

To him who overcomes
I will grant to sit with Me on My throne,
as I also overcame and sat down with My Father on His throne.
Rev. 3:21

He Is A God Of Great Kindness And Comfort

Ps. 145:8	Praise Him for He is full of compassion
Ps. 145:8	Praise Him for He is slow to become angry
Ps. 145:8	Praise Him for He is great in mercy
Ps. 145:9	Praise Him for He is good to everyone
Ps. 69:20	Praise Him when you cannot find a comforter
Jn. 14:18, 21	Praise Him for He will not leave us without comfort
Is. 49:13	Praise Him for He comforts His people (Is. 51:12)
Is. 61:2	Praise Him for He comforts all who mourn
2Cor. 1:3	Praise Him for He comforts us through everything
2Cor. 1:4	Praise Him for He comforts us through every tribulation
2Cor. 1:4	Praise Him for He ministers all His comfort through us
2Cor. 1:5	Praise Him for He increases His comfort in us whenever our suffering increases
2Cor. 1:3	Praise Him for He is the God of all comfort

He Is Kind When You Are In Trouble

Ps. 32:7	Praise Him when you are in trouble
2Cor. 4:8-9	Praise Him when you have trouble on every side
Ps. 71:20	Praise Him when you have been through great and severe trouble yet He revives you and brings you up from the depths of the earth
Ps. 77:4	Praise Him when you are in trouble and cannot speak
2Thess. 1:4	Praise Him when you endure through the trouble
Ps. 77:2	Praise Him when you search for Him in the day of trouble
Ps. 86:7	Praise Him when you call on Him in the day of trouble and He answers you
Ps. 31:7	Praise Him when He knows you in the day of trouble
Ps. 50:15	Praise Him when He delivers you from trouble
Ps. 138:7	Praise Him when He revives you in the midst of trouble
Ps. 46:1-3	Praise Him when He helps you in the midst of trouble
Is. 33:2	Praise Him when He saves you in the day of trouble
Nahum 1:7	Praise Him when He is your stronghold in the day of trouble
Ps. 59:16	Praise Him when He is your refuge in the day of trouble
Ps. 27:5	Praise Him when He hides you in the time of trouble
Ps. 37:39	Praise Him when He is your strength in the time of trouble
Ps. 91:15	Praise Him when He brings honor to you out of your trouble
2Cor. 1:3-4	Praise Him when He comforts you in all your trouble
2Thess. 1:7	Praise Him when He gives you rest from trouble
Ps. 25:15-18	Praise Him when you are in the midst of affliction (Ps. 102:1)
Ex. 5:31	Praise Him when He understands your affliction (Ps. 22:23-24)
Ps. 119:50	Praise Him when His Word is your comfort in affliction
Ps. 34:19	Praise Him when you are delivered out of affliction

Ps. 55:4-8	Praise Him in the midst of the storm (Ps. 81:7)
Is. 25:4	Praise Him when He is a refuge in the storm
Matt. 8:24	Praise Him when He sleeps through the storm
Ps. 107:29	Praise Him when He calms the storm (Job 26:12; Matt. 8:26-27)
Is. 59:19	Praise Him when your enemy comes against you like a flood
Is. 59:19	Praise Him when He lifts up a standard against your enemy
Jas. 1:2	Praise Him when you are in the midst of trials (1Pet. 1:6)
Jas. 1:12	Praise Him when you endure trials (1Pet. 4:13; Rev. 3:10)
Matt. 17:20	Praise Him when you face the impossible
Matt. 19:26	Praise Him when He makes all things possible (Mk. 9:23)
Job 1:21	Praise Him when life is unfair
Ps. 103:10-12	Praise Him when life is better than you deserve
Hab. 3:17-19	Praise Him when you have a terrible season
Job 1:1-22	Praise Him when you have a bad day
Ps. 118:24	Praise Him when you have a great day
Pr. 11:10	Praise Him when things go well

He Is Kind When You Are Discouraged And Without Hope

Ps. 42:5	Praise Him when you are cast down
Ps. 3:3	Praise Him when He lifts your head
Ps. 51:17	Praise Him when you are broken in spirit
Is. 61:1	Praise Him when He heals the brokenhearted (Ps. 147:3)
Ps. 61:2	Praise Him when you are overwhelmed
Ps. 118:15	Praise Him when you are saved

Ps. 42:5, 11	Praise Him when you are in despair
Ps. 40:2	Praise Him when He brings you out of a horrible pit (a pit of despair), out of the miry clay, and He has set your feet upon a rock and has steadied you
Ps. 94:19	Praise Him when you are anxious (Ps. 102:1)
Phil. 4:6	Praise Him when He lifts your anxiety (Jer. 17:8; Lu. 12:22, 29)
Matt. 6:25-34	Praise Him when He tells us not to worry about the details of life
2Cor. 10:12	Praise Him when He tells us not to compare ourselves with others
2Chr. 15:1-5	Praise Him when you have no peace
Ps. 29:11	Praise Him when you find peace
2Thess. 3:16	Praise Him when He gives you His peace (Jn. 14:27)
Is. 26:3	Praise Him when He keeps you in perfect peace
Phil. 4:7	Praise Him when He guards your heart and mind with His peace that passes all understanding
Col. 3:15	Praise Him when His peace fills your heart
1Ki. 8:56	Praise Him when you find His rest
Job 6:11	Praise Him when you have no strength to hope
Lam. 3:18	Praise Him when your hope seems lost (Ez. 37:11)
Zech. 9:12	Praise Him when you are a prisoner of discouragement and He gives you hope and a double portion
Job 14:7	Praise Him when there is glimmer of hope and all seems lost
Is. 57:10	Praise Him when you are very weary yet do not give up hope
Hos. 2:14	Praise Him when He turns your trouble into a door of hope
Ps. 42:5, 11	Praise Him when you choose hope in times of discouragement
Ps. 43:5	Praise Him when you encourage yourself to have hope
Ps. 71:5	Praise Him when you hope from your youth
Rom. 4:18	Praise Him when you have tenacious hope

Lam. 3:21-26	Praise Him when you remember that His mercy and compassion do not fail; when you remember that His faithfulness is new every morning and this causes you to rest in hope
Ps. 119:49	Praise Him when His Word gives you hope (Ps. 119:81, 114, 147; 130:5; Rom. 15:4)
Ps. 38:15	Praise Him when He gives you hope
Ps. 16:9	Praise Him for He gives you hope to rest in (Acts 2:26)
Ps. 71:14	Praise Him when you can hope continually
Jer. 29:11	Praise Him when His thoughts and plans are to give you hope
Ps. 33:18	Praise Him for His eye is on those who hope in Him
Pr. 10:28	Praise Him when your hope results in happiness (Rom. 12:12)
Jer. 17:7	Praise Him for He blesses those who hope in Him
Ps. 31:24	Praise Him for He strengthens the hearts of those who hope in Him
Ps. 147:11	Praise Him for He takes pleasure in those who place their hope in Him
Rom. 5:5	Praise Him for hope will not disappoint you
Rom. 15:13	Praise Him for He is a God of hope who causes you to abound in hope
1Cor. 13:3	Praise Him for He causes your hope to endure
Rom. 5:2	Praise Him when you hope for His glory (Col. 1:27)
Rom. 5:3-4	Praise Him for He can birth hope even in tribulation
Col. 1:5	Praise Him for He has given us a hope for heaven
Joel 3:16	Praise Him for the Lord is our hope and strength
1Tim. 1:1	Praise Him for Christ is our hope
1Pet. 1:21	Praise Him for your hope is in God
1Pet. 1:3	Praise Him for He has given us a living hope through the resurrection of Christ
Ps. 31:24	Praise Him for praise leads us to hope
1Jn. 3:3	Praise Him for hope leads us to holiness
Ps. 43:5	Praise Him when you are sad
Ps. 51	Praise Him when you are bad
Jas. 5:13	Praise Him when you are glad

He Is Kind When You Have No Song

Ps. 137:3-4	Praise Him when you cannot sing
Ps. 40:3	Praise Him when He gives you a new song (Ps. 33:3; 98:1; 118:14)
Is. 35:6	Praise Him when the dumb begin to sing
Lam. 3:14-24	Praise Him when others taunt you with their song
Ps. 42:8	Praise Him when you sing in the night, through the darkness
Hos. 2:15	Praise Him when you sing from the wilderness (Is. 51:3)
Dt. 31:30-32:44	Praise Him when you sing at the end of the wilderness
Acts 16:25	Praise Him when you sing from the prison
2Chr. 20:1-19	Praise Him when you sing before the battle
2Chr. 20:21	Praise Him when you sing in the midst of the battle
2Chr. 20:27-28	Praise Him when you sing at the end of the battle
Ps. 32:7	Praise Him when He surrounds you with songs of deliverance
Zeph. 3:17	Praise Him when He sings over you

He Is Kind When You Have Great Burdens

Matt. 11:28	Praise Him when you are weary and carry heavy burdens
Ps. 55:22	Praise Him when you have burdens and He sustains you
Is. 9:4	Praise Him when He breaks the burden off you (Is. 10:27
Is. 58:6	Praise Him when He lifts all your heavy burdens
Matt. 11:30	Praise Him when He gives you His light burden
1Pet. 2:24	Praise Him for He bore your sins and took your burdens on Himself so that you could live in righteousness
Ps. 118:5	Praise Him when you are distressed (Ps. 18:6)
Ps. 107:6	Praise Him when He delivers you out of your distress
Ps. 118:5	Praise Him when He brings you from distress into a large place

He Is Kind When You Walk Through Difficult Places

Ps. 23:4	Praise Him when you walk through the valley
2Chr. 20:26	Praise Him when you are victorious in the valley
Hos. 2:15	Praise Him when you find peace in the valley
Is. 43:2	Praise Him when you walk through the fire and don't get burned
Dan. 3:20-30	Praise Him when He delivers you in the fire
Ex. 3:2-3	Praise Him when you find Him in the fire (Mark 12:26)
2Chr. 7:3	Praise Him when you see Him come down in fire
Ps. 146:8	Praise Him when He lifts all who are bowed down
Ps. 143:8	Praise Him when He shows you the way to walk
Is. 40:31	Praise Him when He lifts you up to run without becoming weary, and walk without fainting
Is. 42:16	Praise Him when He makes crooked places straight
Is. 40:4	Praise Him when He makes rough places smooth
Matt. 7:14	Praise Him when the way is narrow (Lu. 13:24)
2Sam. 22:37	Praise Him when He makes your path wide so your feet do not slip (Ps. 18:46; 31:8)
Ps. 69:2	Praise Him when you have sunk into deep waters
Ps. 18:16	Praise Him when He rescues you from deep waters (Ps. 69:14-15; 144:7)
Ps. 37:24	Praise Him when you fall
Jude 1:24-25	Praise Him when He keeps you from falling
Ps. 145:14	Praise Him when He upholds you when you fall
Ps. 30:1	Praise Him when you are lifted up (Ps. 3:3)
1Pet. 5:6	Praise Him when He exalts you

Job 12:22	Praise Him when He brings light into the deepest darkness
Ps. 107:24	Praise Him when does wonders in the deepest seas
Lam. 3:55	Praise Him when you call on Him from the lowest pit
Dt. 10:14	Praise Him when you are in the highest heavens
Ps. 57:4	Praise Him when you feel as though you are among lions
Dan. 6:17	Praise Him when you are delivered from the lions
Heb. 11:33	Praise Him when He closes the mouths of lions
1Sam. 17:37	Praise Him when He delivers you from the lion, the bear and the Philistine
Ps. 91:13	Praise Him when you trample lions under your feet
Hos. 11:10	Praise Him when He places His roar in His people
Rev. 5:5	Praise Him when the Lion of Judah prevails
Jonah 2:2, 9	Praise Him when you are in the belly of a fish
Jn. 6:9-11	Praise Him when you are fed with fish
Lu. 5:4-5	Praise Him when He shows you where to fish
Lu. 5:6-7	Praise Him when He fills your net with fish
Lu. 5:10	Praise Him when He makes you a fisher of men
Ps. 66:12	Praise Him when you go through the waters of testing (Ps. 81:7)
Is. 43:2, 16	Praise Him when He walks with you through the waters
Ps. 107:23-24	Praise Him when you sail upon the waters
Ps. 69:1-2	Praise Him when you are overwhelmed by waters (Ps. 124:4-5)
Ex. 15:1-20	Praise Him when He delivers you in the waters
Ps. 18:16	Praise Him when He draws you out of deep waters
Ps. 60:14-15	Praise Him when He delivers you out of the waters
Ps. 23:2	Praise Him when He leads you beside still waters
Ps. 65:7	Praise Him when He stills the waters (Ps. 89:9; 107:29)

| Is. 44:3 | Praise Him when He pours out His water |
| Is. 48:21 | Praise Him when He brings water out of a rock |

| Is. 58:11 | Praise Him when He turns you into a well-watered garden |
| Hab 2:14 | Praise Him when His glory covers the earth like the waters |

| Jn. 4:7-15 | Praise Him when He gives you living water |
| Rev. 22:17 | Praise Him when He calls you to the water of life |

He Is Kind When You Are Weak

2Cor. 12:9	Praise Him when you are weak
Is. 40:29	Praise Him when He gives power to the weak
Ps. 18:32	Praise Him when He arms you with strength
2Cor. 12:10	Praise Him when He makes you strong (Joel 3:10)

Jud. 6:15	Praise Him when you believe you are the weakest
Zech. 12:8	Praise Him when He defends the weakest
1Cor. 12:22	Praise Him when He uses and exalts the weakest

| Is. 42:3 | Praise Him for He will not break you when you are bruised and weak |
| Is. 42:3 | Praise Him for He will not quench you when you are at your weakest and have the smallest hope |

Ps. 73:26	Praise Him when you have no strength
Ps. 71:9	Praise Him when your strength fails
Ps. 71:18	Praise Him when you declare His strength to the next generation
Ps. 138:3	Praise Him when He makes you bold with strength in your soul
Is. 12:2	Praise Him when He becomes your strength
Is. 40:29	Praise Him when He increases your strength
Is. 40:31	Praise Him when He renews your strength
Ex. 15:2	Praise Him when He is your strength and song
Ps. 28:7	Praise Him when He is your strength and shield

He Is Kind When You Need Healing

Ps. 41:3	Praise Him when you are unwell
Lu. 17:15-16	Praise Him when you are healed
	(Jer. 17:14; Matt. 10:1; Lu. 13:13; Acts 3:8)
Jer. 17:14	Praise Him when you cry to Him for healing and He heals you
Ps. 41:3	Praise Him when you are strengthened and sustained in your sickness
Jer. 30:17	Praise Him when He restores your health and heals your wounds
Jas. 5:15	Praise Him when you are sick and the prayer of faith raises you up
Lu. 18:43	Praise Him when you see others healed
Acts 5:15	Praise Him when your shadow falls on people and they are healed
Ps. 63:6	Praise Him when you are on your bed (Ps. 149:5)
Ps. 41:3	Praise Him when He strengthens you on your bed
Mark 2:12	Praise Him when He lifts you out of your bed
Jn. 5:8-9	Praise Him when He tells you to take up your bed and walk
Is. 42:7	Praise Him when He opens blind eyes
	(Ps. 146:8; Matt. 15:30-31; Lu. 4:18)
Ps. 36:9	Praise Him when you see light (2Sam. 22:29)
Is. 29:18	Praise Him when the eyes of the blind see through their gloom and darkness
Matt. 11:5	Praise Him when He heals the deaf
Is. 29:18	Praise Him when the deaf hear the words of the book
Is. 54:1	Praise Him when you are barren (Ps. 113:9)
Ruth 4:13-17	Praise Him when He gives you a child
	(Gen. 29:35; 1Sam. 1:19-2:10)
Is. 44:3	Praise Him when He blesses your children and your children's children

He Is Kind When You Are In Darkness

Is. 30:29	Praise Him when you are in the night
Ps. 119:55	Praise Him when you remember His name in the night
Micah 7:8	Praise Him when you sit in darkness
Job 29:3	Praise Him when you walk through darkness
2Sam. 22:29	Praise Him when He is your lamp in the darkness
2Cor. 4:6	Praise Him when He brings light out of darkness
Is. 42:16	Praise Him when He makes the darkness into light
Ps. 36:9	Praise Him when you are in His light and you see light
Jn. 8:12	Praise Him when He is the light of the world—He takes us out of darkness and gives us the light of life
Ps. 89:15	Praise Him when you are in the light of His countenance (Pr. 16:15)

He Is Kind When You Have People Speaking Against You

Ps. 69:4	Praise Him when you are falsely accused and wrongfully treated (Ps. 119:69)
1Pet. 2:12	Praise Him when people speak against you
Ps. 31:20	Praise Him when He hides you from the tongues of your enemies
Ps. 41:12	Praise Him when He upholds your integrity
Ps. 41:9	Praise Him when you are betrayed (Matt. 24:10; Mk. 14:10; 13:12; 1Cor. 11:23)
Ps. 26:2	Praise Him when you are proven by God even when you have been wronged (Lam. 3:59)
1Pet. 4:16	Praise Him when you suffer persecution as a Christian (Acts 7:59)
Ps. 143:3	Praise Him when your enemy persecutes you and crushes your life (Ps. 119:161)
Ps. 31:16	Praise Him as you are delivered from persecution
1Cor. 4:10	Praise Him when you are an outcast and shamed for Christ's sake

| Micah 4:6-7 | Praise Him when He gathers the outcast and makes them into a strong nation |
| Zeph. 3:19 | Praise Him when He causes the outcast to receive praise wherever they have been shamed |

He Is Kind When You Have Been Put To Shame

Ps. 51	Praise Him when you are ashamed
Ps. 54:1	Praise Him when you are vindicated (Ps. 26:1)
Is. 51:11	Praise Him when you are redeemed (Is. 49:20)

Ps. 69:19-20	Praise Him when you are disgraced
1Cor. 12:26	Praise Him when you are honored
Is. 61:7	Praise Him when He gives you double honor instead of shame

Is. 54:4	Praise Him—He will never put you to shame
Rom. 10:11	Praise Him—He will never put you to shame when you trust in Him
Ps. 119:6	Praise Him—He will never put you to shame when you trust in His Word
2Tim 1:12	Praise Him—He will never put you to shame when you know Him, believe in Him and trust Him

| Ps. 119:22 | Praise Him when He removes reproach from you |
| Josh. 5:9 | Praise Him when He lifts reproach from you |

Ps. 64:1-2	Praise Him when the enemy uncovers you (Ps. 61:3)
Ps. 44:15	Praise Him when you are covered in shame
1Pet. 4:8	Praise Him when Love covers a multitude (all) of sin (Pr. 10:12; 1Pet. 4:8)
Job. 14:17	Praise Him when He covers all your sin (Ps. 32:1; 85:2; Rom. 4:7)
Ez. 16:8	Praise Him when He covers your nakedness
Ruth 3:9	Praise Him when He covers you as your nearest kinsman
Ps. 139:13	Praise Him when He covers you in your mother's womb
Ps. 140:7	Praise Him when He covers your head in battle

Is. 61:3	Praise Him when He covers you with garments of praise
Is. 61:10	Praise Him when He covers you with garments of salvation
Is. 61:10	Praise Him when He covers you with garments of righteousness and justice (Job 29:14)
Pr. 31:25	Praise Him when He covers you with garments of strength and honor
Ps. 30:11	Praise Him when He covers you with garments of joy
1Pet. 5:5	Praise Him when He covers you with humility
Ez. 16:10, 18	Praise Him when He covers you with fine linen, silk, and embroidered garments
Ps. 91:4	Praise Him when He covers you with His feathers
Ex. 33:22	Praise Him when He covers you with His hand (Is. 51:16)

He Is Kind When You Are Weeping

Ps. 30:11	Praise Him when you are mourning (Is. 61:3)
Ps. 126:6	Praise Him when you weep
Ps. 6:6	Praise Him when you are drenched with tears
Is. 38:5	Praise Him when He sees your tears
Rev. 21:4	Praise Him when He wipes away every tear (Is. 25:8)
Lu. 7:38	Praise Him when you wash Him with your tears
Ps. 56:8	Praise Him when He gathers your tears to remember them
Ps. 116:8	Praise Him when He delivers you from tears
Ps. 126:6	Praise Him when He causes you to rejoice
Ps. 126:2	Praise Him when He fills your mouth with laughter

He Is Kind When You Have No Family Or Friends

Ps. 27:10	Praise Him when your father and mother forsake you
Ps. 37:25	Praise Him when you realize He will never forsake you
Ps. 146:9	Praise Him when He comforts the fatherless
Dt. 10:18	Praise Him when He gives justice to the fatherless
Hos. 14:3	Praise Him when He is merciful to the fatherless
Ps. 68:5	Praise Him when He is a Father to the fatherless

Rom. 8:14-15	Praise Him when He has adopts us
2Cor. 6:18	Praise Him when He is our Father
Jn. 1:12	Praise Him when He calls us sons (1Jn. 3:1-2)
Heb. 2:6	Praise Him when He takes care of us

1Tim. 5:5	Praise Him when you are a widow
Dt. 10:18	Praise Him when He gives justice to the widow (Ps. 68:5)
Pr. 15:25	Praise Him when He prospers the widow
Jer. 49:11	Praise Him when He is trustworthy for the widow
Hos. 2:16	Praise Him when He becomes your husband

Ps. 146:9	Praise Him when you are a stranger
Ps. 146:9	Praise Him when He preserves the strangers
Dt. 10:18	Praise Him when He provides for the strangers

| Pr. 27:6 | Praise Him when your friend wounds you in love |
| Pr. 31:12 | Praise Him when He wounds you in love (Heb. 12:6) |

Ps. 41:9	Praise Him even when your friends turn on you
Jn. 15:13-15	Praise Him for He has made us His friends
Dt. 31:6	Praise Him for He will never leave you alone (Jn. 14:18)
Ps. 68:6	Praise Him when He places the lonely into families

He Is Kind When You Are Hungry, Thirsty And Have Nothing

Phil. 4:12	Praise Him when you are hungry
Ps. 146:7	Praise Him when He gives food to the hungry
Matt. 6:11	Praise Him when He provides food for each day
Ps. 107:9	Praise Him when He fills the hungry with goodness
Matt. 15:32-38	Praise Him when He miraculously feeds the hungry
Is. 58:7, 10	Praise Him when you share with the hungry

Ps. 143:6	Praise Him when you are thirsty
Ps. 63:1	Praise Him when you are in the desert
Is. 58:11	Praise Him when you are satisfied and strengthened in the desert
Is. 43:19-20	Praise Him when He provides rivers of water in the desert

Ps. 42:1	Praise Him when you long and thirst for water (Ps. 63:1)
Num. 21:16-18	Praise Him when He provides you with water
Ps. 42:2	Praise Him when you thirst for Him

Jer. 20:13	Praise Him when you are poor and needy (Ps. 74:21)
Ps. 69:33	Praise Him when He hears the poor
Ps. 113:7	Praise Him when He raises the poor from the dust
Jer. 20:13	Praise Him when He delivers the poor
Is. 25:4	Praise Him when He is a strength to the poor and needy
Ps. 12:5	Praise Him when He give justice to the poor (Ps. 72:4, 14; 109:31)
Ps. 132:15	Praise Him when He satisfies the poor with bread
Is. 55:1	Praise Him when you have no money and He provides abundant refreshing and food
Ps. 115:14	Praise Him when He generously provides (2Cor. 8:9)
Ps. 22:29	Praise Him when you prosper (Eccl. 7:14)
Ps. 37:11	Praise Him when you inherit the earth

Lu. 11:6	Praise Him when you have nothing
1Chr. 29:11	Praise Him for everything in heaven and earth is His
Rom. 8:32	Praise Him when He gives you everything (Ps. 23:1)

He Is Kind When You Walk Away From Sin

Heb. 4:15-16	Praise Him when you are tempted
Heb. 2:18	Praise Him when He helps you when you are tempted
Matt. 4:1-11	Praise Him when you overcome temptation
Matt. 6:13	Praise Him when He keeps you from temptation
1Cor. 10:13	Praise Him when He leads you out of temptation
2Pet. 2:9	Praise Him when He delivers you from temptation

Ps. 79:9	Praise Him when you seek forgiveness
Ps. 130:3-4	Praise Him when you find forgiveness
Matt. 6:12, 14	Praise Him when you forgive others who have sinned against you—then He will forgive you also

Ez. 16:9	Praise Him when He washes and anoints you
Eph. 5:26	Praise Him when He washes you with the Word
Titus 3:5	Praise Him when He washes you with the Holy Spirit
Rev. 1:5	Praise Him when you are washed with His blood (Rev. 7:14)
Ps. 51:2	Praise Him when He washes you from sin (1Cor. 6:11)
Ps. 51:7	Praise Him when He washes you whiter than snow
Ps. 103:12	Praise Him when He removes your sin as far as the east is from the west
Jn. 13:5	Praise Him when He washes your feet
Lu. 7:38	Praise Him when you wash His feet with your tears, and anoint Him with fragrant oil
Ps. 97:12	Praise Him when you are righteous (Ps. 51:19; 68:3; 118:19)
Ps. 118:19	Praise Him in the gates of righteousness
Job 33:26	Praise Him when you are restored to righteousness
Is. 55:7	Praise Him when you turn from unrighteousness
Jer. 15:19	Praise Him for He restores you so that you can speak precious and worthy things from the places where you once were unworthy and vile
Acts 16:25	Praise Him when you are in prison
Heb. 11:36	Praise Him when you are tortured in prison
Heb. 13:3	Praise Him when you intercede for those in prison
Is. 61:1	Praise Him when He opens the prison
Ps. 146:7	Praise Him for He gives freedom to prisoners
Ps. 142:7	Praise Him when you get out of prison
Is. 42:7	Praise Him when He brings you out of the darkest prison
Ps. 107:10	Praise Him when you are bound in chains (Col. 4:3)
Ps. 107:14	Praise Him when He breaks your chains in pieces (Acts 16:26)
Ps. 149:8	Praise Him when He binds evil kings with chains
Lu. 8:26-39	Praise Him when He sets men free who have been bound with demons and chains (Mk. 5:1-20)

Acts 12:6-7	Praise Him when angels break your chains and set you free
Rev. 20:1-2	Praise Him when He places the devil in chains for a thousand years
Ps. 51:12	Praise Him when He restores the joy of your salvation
Ps. 80:3, 7, 19	Praise Him when He shines His face on you and restores you
Ps. 119:107	Praise Him when His Word restores you
Joel 2:25	Praise Him when He restores the years that the locust has eaten
Zech. 9:12	Praise Him when He restores double after your shame
Gal. 6:1	Praise Him when He restores you after you have sinned
Heb. 12:12	Praise Him when He restores you after you have been discouraged

Chapter Ten

Praise Him For He Builds Us Up

For the Lamb who is in the midst of the throne will shepherd them
and lead them to living fountains of waters.
And God will wipe away every tear from their eyes
Rev. 7:17

He Hears And Knows Us

Ps. 77:1	Praise Him when you cry out to Him (Ps. 18:6)
Ps. 5:3	Praise Him when He hears your cry (Ps. 22:24)
Ps. 18:3	Praise Him when you call for Him (Ps. 55:16)
Jer. 33:3	Praise Him when He answers your call (Ps. 50:15; 86:7; 91:15; Is. 58:9; Jer. 33:3)
Ps. 5:1-3	Praise Him when He hears your voice
Jn. 10:27	Praise Him when you recognize His voice
Ps. 121:1	Praise Him when you are looking for help
Ps. 121:2	Praise Him when He is your help
Ps. 139:1	Praise Him when He knows everything about you
Ex. 33:12	Praise Him when He knows you by name
Ps. 144:3	Praise Him when He thinks about you
Heb. 10:22	Praise Him when you can draw near to Him because you are washed by Him (Jas. 4:8)
Ps. 73:28	Praise Him when you can trust in Him (Ps. 5:11; 64:10; 118:8)
Phil. 3:10	Praise Him when you can know Him
Jn. 4:22	Praise Him when you know nothing
Dan. 2:20, 23	Praise Him when He gives you wisdom and might

He Gives Us New Life

Ps. 16:11	Praise Him for He shows you the path of life
Ps. 27:1	Praise Him for He is the strength of your life
Ps. 36:9	Praise Him for He is a fountain of life
Ps. 63:3	Praise Him for His lovingkindness is better than life
Ps. 103:4	Praise Him for He redeems your life
Ps. 119:50	Praise Him for His Word gives you life
Jn. 1:4	Praise Him for His life gives you light
Pr. 3:18	Praise Him for His wisdom becomes a tree of life
Pr. 14:27	Praise Him for the fear of God is a fountain of life
1Jn. 3:16	Praise Him for He laid down His life for you
Jn. 3:16	Praise Him for He gives you everlasting life
Jn. 12:25	Praise Him for you lose your life to gain His life
Rom. 6:4	Praise Him for you walk in newness of life
Col. 3:3	Praise Him for your life is hidden with Christ in God
Jas. 1:12	Praise Him for you will receive the crown of life
Rev. 20:12	Praise Him for your name is in the book of life

He Turns Us Into Overcomers

Jn. 16:33	Praise Him for He is has overcome the world
1Jn. 5:4-5	Praise Him for He gives you the power to overcome the world through your faith
Num. 13:30	Praise Him for you are able to overcome all enemies
1Jn. 4:4	Praise Him for He who is in you is greater than he who is in the world, and He helps you to overcome all evil
1Jn. 2:13	Praise Him for you can overcome the devil
Rom. 12:21	Praise Him for you can overcome evil with good
1Cor. 15:57	Praise Him for He gives you victory and strength to overcome through Jesus Christ
2Cor. 2:14	Praise Him for He leads you in triumphant procession as an overcomer
Rev. 2:7	Praise Him for all those who overcome will eat from the tree of life
Rev. 2:11	Praise Him for all those who overcome will not die
Rev. 2:17	Praise Him for all those who overcome will receive hidden manna

Rev. 2:26	Praise Him for all those who overcome will receive power over nations
Rev. 3:5	Praise Him for all those who overcome will receive white garments
Rev. 3:5	Praise Him for all those who overcome will not have their names blotted out from the Book of Life
Rev. 3:5	Praise Him for all those who overcome will have their names called out before the Father and the angels
Rev. 3:12	Praise Him for all those who overcome will become a pillar in the temple of God
Rev. 3:12	Praise Him for all those who overcome will have His new name written on them
Rev. 3:21	Praise Him for all those who overcome will sit with Him on His throne
Rev. 21:7	Praise Him for all those who overcome will inherit all things
Rev. 21:7	Praise Him for all those who overcome will be His sons, and He will be their God

He Turns Everything Around

Neh. 13:2	Praise Him for He turns our curses into blessings
Esther 9:22	Praise Him for He turns our sorrow into joy
Jer. 31:13	Praise Him for He turns our mourning into joy
Ps. 30:11	Praise Him for He turns our mourning into dancing
Ps. 18:28	Praise Him for He turns our darkness into light
Ps. 107:35	Praise Him for He turns our wilderness into pools of water (Is. 41:18)
Hos. 2:14-15	Praise Him for He turns our wilderness into vineyards
Hos. 2:15	Praise Him for He turns our trouble into doors of hope
Amos 9:14	Praise Him for He turns our captivity into prosperity
Mal. 4:6	Praise Him for He turns our hearts toward our children and our children's hearts toward us
Lu. 1:17	Praise Him for He turns our disobedience into wisdom
1Ki. 18:37	Praise Him for He turns hearts back to His presence

He Is Near

.

Ps. 22:11	Praise Him when trouble is near
Ps. 34:18	Praise Him when He is near (Ps. 119:151; 245:18)
Ps. 75:1	Praise Him when His name is near
Ps. 85:9	Praise Him when His salvation is near
Ps. 73:28	Praise Him when you draw near to Him
Jas. 4:8	Praise Him when He draws near to you and you draw near to Him
Eph. 2:13	Praise Him when His blood makes us to be near
Rev. 1:3	Praise Him when the time for His return is very near
Ps. 91:7, 10	Praise Him when trouble cannot come near you

He Helps Us Find Everything We Need

Ex. 33:13	Praise Him when you find grace in His sight
Pr. 3:3-4	Praise Him when you find favor in His sight
Pr. 2:3-6	Praise Him when you find the knowledge of God
Pr. 3:13	Praise Him when you find wisdom (Pr. 8:17)
Pr. 21:21	Praise Him when you find life, righteousness and honor
Is. 40:31	Praise Him when you find new strength as you wait on Him
Jer. 6:16	Praise Him when you find rest for your soul by walking in goodly paths
Matt. 11:25	Praise Him when you find rest for your soul by taking His yoke upon yourself
Matt. 7:14	Praise Him when you find the narrow gate and path to life
Matt. 10:39	Praise Him when you find life by giving up your life for Him
Heb 4:15	Praise Him when you find grace in times of need
Matt. 7:7	Praise Him when you ask and He gives you what you have asked for
Matt. 7:7	Praise Him when you seek and He shows you what you are looking for
Matt. 7:7	Praise Him when you knock and He opens the door for you

He Builds Us Up In Faith

Matt. 5:3	Praise Him when you are poor in spirit—when you realize your need of Him and He gives you the kingdom of heaven
Matt. 5:4	Praise Him when you mourn and He comforts you
Matt. 5:5	Praise Him when you are meek (gentle and lowly) and He gives you an inheritance of the whole earth
Matt. 5:6	Praise Him when you hunger and thirst for righteousness (justice) and He fills you with it
Matt. 5:7	Praise Him when you are merciful to others and He is merciful to you
Matt. 5:8	Praise Him when you are pure in your heart and He allows you to see His glory
Matt. 5:9	Praise Him when you work for peace and He calls you His sons
Matt. 5:10	Praise Him when you are persecuted because you live for God and He gives you the kingdom of heaven
Matt. 5:11-12	Praise Him when others mock, persecute and lie about you because you follow the Lord for He will reward you greatly
2Cor. 5:7	Praise Him when you walk by faith
Gal. 2:20; 3:11	Praise Him when you live by faith
2Cor. 8:7	Praise Him when you abound in faith
1Thess. 1:3	Praise Him when you grow in faith
1Tim. 6:11	Praise Him when you pursue faith
1Tim. 6:12	Praise Him when you fight in faith
2Tim. 3:10	Praise Him when you follow faith
2Tim. 4:7	Praise Him when you keep the faith
Jas. 5:15	Praise Him when you pray in faith
Jude 1:3	Praise Him when you contend for faith
Gal. 2:16	Praise Him when you are justified by faith
Eph. 2:8	Praise Him when you are saved by faith
Col. 2:7	Praise Him when you are established in faith
1Tim. 3:13	Praise Him when you are bold in faith
1Tim. 4:12	Praise Him when you are an example in faith
Jas. 2:5	Praise Him when you are rich in faith
2Tim. 3:15	Praise Him when you are made wise through faith
Jas. 1:3	Praise Him when you are made patient through faith

1Jn. 5:4	Praise Him when you overcome the world through faith
Jude 1:20	Praise Him when you build yourself up in faith
Heb. 11:6	Praise Him when you please Him and come to Him through faith
Matt. 17:20	Praise Him when you have faith that moves mountains
Eph. 3:17	Praise Him for He dwells in you through faith
Rom. 8:34	Praise Him for He intercedes for you (Heb. 7:25)

He Brings Us To Holiness

Amos 5:14	Praise Him when you seek good
Joel 2:12-13	Praise Him when you turn to the Lord
Ez. 36:26	Praise Him for He gives us a new heart—a heart of flesh instead of a heart of stone
Is. 6:3	Praise Him when you behold Him who is holy
Heb. 12:14	Praise Him when you seek holiness
Ob. 1:17	Praise Him when you come to holiness
Rom. 6:19	Praise Him when you become a slave to holiness
Rom. 6:22	Praise Him when you have the fruit of holiness
2Cor. 7:1	Praise Him when you perfect holiness
1Pet. 1:15-16	Praise Him when you become holy
1Thess. 3:13	Praise Him when you are established in holiness
1Thess. 4:4	Praise Him when you live in holiness and honor
Rev. 22:11	Praise Him when you continue in holiness
1Chr. 16:29	Praise Him in the beauty and splendor of holiness (Ps. 29:2; 96:9)
Is. 35:8	Praise Him for He has set us on a highway of holiness
Heb. 12:10	Praise Him for His discipline leads us to holiness
Ez. 36:23	Praise Him for He will reveal His holiness in us and through us to the nations

Chapter Eleven

Praise Him In The Fear Of God

Then a voice came from the throne, saying,
"Praise our God, all you His servants and those who fear Him,
both small and great!"
Rev. 19:5

This chapter is very much linked to Chapter Nine in that it deals with negative circumstances that are dealt with in the light of His graciousness. It is important to know that the fear of God is entirely different from being afraid of God. The fear of God has three basic components:

- To know Him
- To worship Him
- To obey Him

The fear of man will keep you from the fear of God—the fear of God will keep you from the fear of man (Pr. 29:25)

When You Are Afraid

Ps. 56:3	Praise Him when you are afraid (Ps. 27:1)
Is. 38:20	Praise Him when you fear man (Is. 41:13)
	Praise Him when you are afraid—He holds your hand and helps you
Ps. 34:4	Praise Him when He delivers you from fear
Ps. 56:4	Praise Him when you are not afraid of anything man can do to you (Heb. 13:6)
Jn. 14:27	Praise Him for He gives you peace instead of fear

2Tim. 1:7	Praise Him for God has not given us a spirit of fear and timidity, but of power, love, and self-discipline
Is. 54:14	Praise Him for you do not need to be afraid

The Fear Of God

Ps. 22:23	Praise Him when you fear God
Ex. 15:11	Praise Him for He is fearful in praises
Rev. 14:7	Praise Him and fear Him for He is a just God
Rev. 15:4	Praise Him and fear Him all nations and all people
Mal. 3:16	Praise Him for He hears those who fear Him and writes their names in His book
Ps. 145:19	Praise Him for He fulfills the desires of those who fear Him
Ps. 145:19	Praise Him for He hears the cry of those who fear Him and He saves them
Ps. 147:11	Praise Him for He takes pleasure in those who fear Him
Ps. 85:9	Praise Him for His salvation is near those who fear Him
Ps. 115:13	Praise Him for He blesses those who fear Him
Pr. 16:6	Praise Him for He teaches those who fear Him to turn from evil
Lu. 1:50	Praise Him for His mercy is for those who fear Him
Ps. 33:18	Praise Him for His eyes are on all those who fear Him
Ps. 25:14	Praise Him for His secrets are given to those who fear Him
Eccl. 8:12	Praise Him for all goes well for those who fear Him (Dt. 5:29)
Pr. 22:4	Praise Him for He grants riches, honor and life to those who fear Him (Ps. 15:4)
Dt. 6:2	Praise Him for He gives longer life to those who fear Him (Pr. 10:27; 19:23)
Acts 13:26	Praise Him when you fear Him and you hear of His salvation
Ps. 128:1	Praise Him when you fear Him and you are able to walk in His ways

2Cor. 7:1	Praise Him when you fear Him and you are able to perfect holiness
Pr. 14:26	Praise Him when you fear Him and you gain confidence
Pr. 14:26	Praise Him when you fear Him and you come across a place of refuge
Pr. 14:27	Praise Him when you fear Him and you find a fountain of life
Pr. 3:7-8	Praise Him when you fear Him and you become healthy (Mal. 4:2)
Ps. 31:19	Praise Him when you fear Him and you find His great goodness
Ps. 25:14	Praise Him when you fear Him and you discover His secrets
Is. 33:6	Praise Him you fear Him and you learn the key to His treasure
Ps. 103:11, 17	Praise Him when you fear Him and you receive His mercy (Lu. 1:50)
Ps. 103:13	Praise Him when you fear Him and you receive His compassion
Ps. 111:10	Praise Him when you fear Him and you come into His wisdom (Pr. 9:10; 15:33)
Ps. 34:7	Praise Him when you fear Him and you know that angels are stationed all around you
Ps. 34:9	Praise Him when you fear Him and you have no need
2Ki. 17:39	Praise Him when you fear Him and He delivers you from all your enemies
Rev. 11:18	Praise Him when you fear Him and He rewards you
Acts 10:35	Praise Him and fear Him all nations, then He will accept you
Rev. 15:4	Praise Him and fear Him all nations, for He alone is holy
Eccl. 12:13	Praise Him and fear Him for this is the whole duty of every man
Ps. 25:14	Praise Him for His secrets are given to those who fear Him
Pr. 3:32	Praise Him for His secrets are given to the righteous
Amos 3:7	Praise Him for His secrets are given to prophets

The Victory You Have In God

Ps. 27:3	Praise Him when an army comes against you
2Sam. 22:30	Praise Him when you can overtake an entire troop
2Chr. 20:21	Praise Him when you can defeat an overwhelming army by praising God
2Chr. 20:17	Praise Him when He fights on your behalf
Rom. 8:31	Praise Him when God is for you and no one can stand against you
Ps. 7:6	Praise Him when your enemies rage against you
Ps. 27:2-5	Praise Him when your enemies come against you
Ps. 25:19	Praise Him when your enemies are many and are very cruel
Ps. 38:19	Praise Him when your enemies are multiplied and very strong
Ps. 69:4	Praise Him when your enemies hate you without cause and you are forced to restore what you did not steal
Ps. 102:8	Praise Him when your enemies speak against you all day long (Ps. 71:10; 102:8)
Lam. 1:21	Praise Him when your enemies hear of your trouble and rejoice in your suffering
Lam. 3:52	Praise Him when your enemies hunt you down without cause
1Sam. 2:1	Praise Him when you can smile at your enemies because of His salvation
Ps. 18:1, 3	Praise Him when you are delivered from your enemies (2Sam. 22:1, 4; Ps. 31:15; 59:1)
Ps. 9:3	Praise Him when your enemies fall and perish at His presence
Ps. 18:3, 48	Praise Him when you call on the Lord and are saved from your enemies
Ps. 23:5	Praise Him when He prepares a table for you in the presence of your enemies
Ps. 25:2	Praise Him when He will not allow your enemies to triumph over you
Ps. 27:6	Praise Him when He lifts your head above your enemies

Ps. 27:11	Praise Him when He leads you on a smooth path in the face of your enemies
Ps. 41:2	Praise Him when He stands against the will of your enemies
Ps. 119:98	Praise Him when He makes you wiser than your enemies through His Word
Ps. 143:9	Praise Him when He is a shelter from your enemies
Micah 7:8	Praise Him when the lifts you and gives you light in the face of your enemies
2Ki. 17:39	Praise Him when He delivers you from the hand of all your enemies
Zeph. 3:14-15	Praise Him when He turns back your enemies

The Protection Of God As You Walk In Him

1Sam. 19:11	Praise Him when others watch your life in order to destroy you (Ps. 56:6; 59:3; 71:10)
Ps. 121:4, 7-8	Praise Him when He watches over your life and keeps you from harm.
Ps. 4:8	Praise Him when He watches over you while you sleep (Pr. 3:24)
1Pet. 3:12	Praise Him when He watches over you when you are right with Him
Ps. 128:1	Praise Him when you fear Him and you are able to walk in His ways—then you will be blessed (Hos. 14:9)
Dt. 5:33; 8:6	Praise Him when you walk in all His ways and fear Him (Jer. 7:23)
Ps. 89:15, 16	Praise Him when you walk in the light of His countenance and rejoice all day
Ps. 26:11	Praise Him when you walk in integrity
Ps. 84:11	Praise Him when you walk uprightly
Ps. 119:1	Praise Him when you walk in the law
Ps. 119:35	Praise Him when you walk in the path of His commands
Pr. 2:20	Praise Him when you walk in goodness
Is. 2:3	Praise Him when you walk in His paths
Ez. 11:20	Praise Him when you walk in His statutes
Micah 4:5	Praise Him when you walk in His name

Rom. 6:4	Praise Him when you walk in newness of life
2Cor. 5:7	Praise Him when you walk in faith (Rom. 4:12)
Gal. 5:16	Praise Him when you walk in the Spirit—you overcome the flesh (Gal. 5:25; Eph. 4:1)
Eph. 5:2	Praise Him when you walk in love
Col. 2:6	Praise Him when you walk in Christ
Col. 4:5	Praise Him when you walk in wisdom (Eph. 5:15)
1Jn. 1:7	Praise Him when you walk in the light (Is. 2:5)
1Jn. 1:6	Praise Him when you walk in obedience
3Jn. 1:3-4	Praise Him when you walk in the truth
Ps. 3:5	Praise Him for He protects and sustains us
Ps. 18:35	Praise Him for He holds us up with His right hand
Ps. 40:11	Praise Him for He continually preserves us
Ps. 125:2	Praise Him for He surrounds us forever
Ps. 18:2	Praise Him for He is our stronghold
Ps. 18:18	Praise Him for He is our support
Ps. 18:30	Praise Him for He is our shield
Ps. 27:1	Praise Him for He is our strength
Ps. 32:7	Praise Him for He is our hiding place
Ps. 28:8	Praise Him for He is our refuge
Ps. 91:4	Praise Him for He is our covering
Ps. 91:2	Praise Him for He is our fortress
Ps. 121:5	Praise Him for He is our shade
Ps. 20:1	Praise Him for He is our defender
Ps. 25:20	Praise Him for He is our keeper
Ps. 31:1	Praise Him for He is our deliverer
Ps. 33:20	Praise Him for He is our helper
Ps. 35:17	Praise Him for He is our rescuer
Ps. 61:4	Praise Him for He is our shelter
Ps. 121:5	Praise Him for He is our keeper
Ps. 144:2	Praise Him for He is our high tower
Pr. 2:8	Praise Him for He is our guard (2Thess. 3:3)
Is. 58:8	Praise Him for He is our rear guard
Phil. 4:7	Praise Him for His peace, which passes understanding will guard our hearts and minds

Chapter Twelve

Praise Him All Peoples and Creatures

*After these things I looked, and behold, a great multitude which no
one could number, of all nations, tribes, peoples,
and tongues, standing before the throne and before the Lamb, clothed
with white robes, with palm branches in their hands*
Rev. 7:9

Praise Him All Heavens And Earth

Ps. 148:3	Praise Him sun, moon and stars
Is. 49:13	Praise Him heavens (Ps. 69:34; Is. 44:23)
Ps. 148:4	Praise Him heaven of heavens
Ps. 148:4	Praise Him waters above the heavens
Ps. 69:34	Praise Him seas
Ps. 148:7	Praise Him sea creatures (Ps. 69:34)
Ps. 98:7	Praise Him seas and waves (1Chr. 16:32)
Is. 42:10	Praise Him coastlands (Is. 24:15)
Ps. 97:1	Praise Him Islands (Is. 42:10, 12)
Ps. 148:8	Praise Him fire, hail, snow, clouds and stormy winds
Ps. 14:9	Praise Him fruitful trees and all cedars
Ps. 148:10	Praise Him Beasts and all cattle; Creeping things and flying fowl
Ps. 84:3	Praise Him birds (Ps. 104:12)
Is. 14:7	Praise Him all the earth (Ps. 66:4; 69:34)
Phil. 2:10	Praise Him on the earth
Is. 44:23	Praise Him lower parts of the earth
Phil. 2:10	Praise Him under the earth
Is. 48:20	Praise Him to the ends of the earth (Ps. 48:10)
Is. 49:13	Praise Him Mountains (Ps. 148:9)
Ps. 98:8	Praise Him hills
Ps. 98:8	Praise Him rivers

Is. 52:9	Praise Him waste places
Is. 55:12	Praise Him trees and forests (Is. 44:23)

Praise Him All People

Is. 52:8	Praise Him watchmen
Ps. 148:11	Praise Him all peoples
Is. 61:11	Praise Him all nations (Ps. 86:9; Jer. 50:2)
Is. 25:3	Praise Him strong nations
Ps. 72:11	Praise Him all kings (Ps. 102:15)
Ps. 148:2	Praise Him angels and hosts (Ps. 103:21; Heb. 1:6)
Rev. 4:9	Praise Him living creatures
Rev. 4:10	Praise Him elders (Rev. 7:11)
Rev. 19:5	Praise Him all servants
Rev. 19:5	Praise Him all who fear Him
Rev. 19:5	Praise Him small and great
Is. 66:23	Praise Him all flesh (Is. 45:23; 66:23)
Is. 12:6	Praise Him inhabitants of Zion
Zeph. 3:14	Praise Him daughter of Zion (Zech. 2:10)
Is. 51:11	Praise Him redeemed of the Lord
Ps. 32:11	Praise Him you who are upright in heart
Ps. 118:15	Praise Him you who are righteous
Ps. 79:13	Praise Him you sheep of His pasture
Ps. 8:2	Praise Him babes and nursing infants
Ps. 148:12	Praise Him young men and maidens
Ps. 148:12	Praise Him old men and children
Lu. 2:20	Praise Him shepherds
Rom. 15:11	Praise Him all Gentiles
Ps. 34:3	Praise Him together

Praise Him All Generations And Nations

Ps. 24:6	Praise Him when your generation seeks Him
Ps. 45:17	Praise Him from one generation to the next (Ps. 78:4-6; 79:13; 89:1, 4; 100:5; 135:13; 145:4; 146:10)
Ps. 102:18	Praise Him in the generations to come (Ps. 78:4)
Ps. 79:13	Praise Him to all generations

Ps. 119:9	Praise Him when you are young (Eccl. 11:9)
Lam. 2:19	Praise Him when your youngest are suffering
1Sam. 17:14	Praise Him when He uses the youngest for His glory
Mk. 9:36-37	Praise Him when He gathers the young to Himself
Acts 2:17	Praise Him when your youngest begin to minister (1Tim. 4:12)
Ps. 37:25	Praise Him when you have been young but now are old and remember His faithfulness (Ps. 71:9, 18; Jer. 31:13)
Ps. 92:14	Praise Him when you bear fruit in old age
Gen. 18:18	Praise Him when He blesses the nations (Gal. 3:8)
Zech. 8:22-23	Praise Him when He speaks to the nations
Ps. 22:27-28	Praise Him when He rules the nations (Ps. 47:8; 67:4)
Pr. 14:34	Praise Him when He exalts the nations
Mal. 1:11	Praise Him when He exalts His name in the nations
Ps. 46:10	Praise Him when He is exalted in the nations
Jn. 12:32	Praise Him when He is lifted up before the nations
Ps. 113:4	Praise Him when He is high above the nations
Is. 56:7	Praise Him when He prays for the nations
Is. 5:26	Praise Him when He whistles to the nations
Is. 5:26	Praise Him when He gathers the nations (Is. 11:12; 66:18)
Ps. 2:4	Praise Him when He laughs at the nations (Ps. 59:8)
Is. 45:1	Praise Him when He subdues the nations
Ps. 94:10	Praise Him when He instructs the nations
Ps. 110:6	Praise Him when He judges the nations
Matt. 12:18	Praise Him when He gives justice to the nations (Is. 51:4)
Hag. 2:6-9	Praise Him when He shakes the nations
Ps. 47:3	Praise Him when He defeats the nations
Ps. 82:8	Praise Him when He inherits the nations
Jer. 10:7	Praise Him when He is King of the nations
Ps. 2:8	Praise Him when He gives you the nations
2Chr. 7:14	Praise Him when He forgives the nations
Rev. 22:2	Praise Him when He heals the nations
Dt. 26:19	Praise Him when He sets you high above the nations
Rom. 16:26-27	Praise Him when He sends His Word to the nations
Matt. 24:14	Praise Him when He sends His gospel to the nations

Ps. 102:15	Praise Him when He is feared among the nations
Rev. 7:9	Praise Him when He is worshiped by all the nations (Rev. 15:4; Ps. 22:27-28; 86:9)
Is. 61:11	Praise Him when He causes righteousness and praise to spring up like flowers before the nations
Acts 15:16-17	Praise Him when He restores the Tabernacle of David so that all the nations may seek Him (Amos 9:11-12)
Ps. 33:10	Praise Him for He brings the counsel of the nations to nothing; He nullifies all their schemes
Ps. 33:11	Praise Him for His counsel stands forever—even to all generations
Rom. 14:11	Praise Him with every knee bowing and every tongue confessing that He is Lord

Praise Him With All The Great Saints Throughout The Bible

This list is a small sampling of some of my favorite Bible characters. I have listed them in chronological order—not the order they are found in the Bible. I don't have any proof, but perhaps the praises of these great men and women continue to resound through the airwaves, and throughout all the ages just like the ripples of a pebble that is dropped into a pool of water. All that is needed is for us to join our hearts and voices with theirs and fill the earth with praise that is due the Lord.

Gen. 1-2	Praise Him with **Adam** and **Eve** who walked with God
Gen. 4:17-5:24	Praise Him with **Enoch** who never died
Gen. 5:29-9:29	Praise Him with **Noah** who obeyed God and was selected out of his generation to save all living things
Gen. 14:13-25:8	Praise Him with **Abraham** who offered his only son to God in worship, and who was the father of many nations (Heb. 11:17-19)
Heb. 11:11	Praise Him with **Sarah** who had faith to birth a son in her old age
Gen. 17-35	Praise God with **Isaac** who was the child of promise
Gen. 32	Praise Him with **Jacob** who wrestled with God and fathered the 12 tribes of Israel

Gen. 41	Praise Him with **Joseph** who rose from slavery and prison to become Prime Minister of Egypt
Job	Praise Him with **Job** who was blameless and upright
Ex.-Dt.	Praise Him with **Moses** who led Israel out of Egypt and saw God face to face like a friend
Ex.-Dt.	Praise Him with **Aaron,** the first high priest in Israel
Joshua	Praise Him with **Joshua** who brought down the walls of Jericho and led Israel into the Promised Land
Judges 4-5	Praise Him with **Deborah** a prophetic leader of Israel who helped defeat the Canaanites
Judges 6-8	Praise Him with **Gideon** who defeated the Midianites
Judges 13-16	Praise Him with **Samson** who used his mighty strength to win many victories over the Philistines
1Samuel 1-28	Praise Him with **Samuel** who was a great prophet and judge of Israel
Ruth	Praise Him with **Ruth** who through faithfulness became the great-grandmother of David
Psalms	Praise Him with **David**, the greatest king of Israel who wrote glorious praises, and was the only one in the Bible who was called "a man after God's own heart" (1Sam. 13:14; Acts 13:22)
Proverbs	Praise Him with **Solomon** who served God with uncommon wisdom
1Ki. 17-2Ki. 2:11	Praise Him with **Elijah** who was one of the most famous and dramatic prophets of Israel
1Ki. 19-2Ki. 13	Praise Him with **Elisha** who impacted four nations —Israel, Judah, Moab, Syria—with his miracles and prophecies
2Chr. 20	Praise Him with **Jehoshaphat** who led Judah in glorious victory using singers of praise
Jonah 2	Praise Him with **Jonah** who cried out to God from the belly of a great fish
Hosea	Praise Him with **Hosea** who demonstrated God's love for Israel
Isaiah	Praise Him with **Isaiah** who saw the Lord high and lifted up and was considered the greatest Old Testament prophet
2Chr. 28-32	Praise Him with **Hezekiah** who led a revival of worship

Jeremiah	Praise Him with **Jeremiah** a prophet who was a catalyst for the great spiritual reformation under King Josiah
Daniel	Praise Him with **Daniel** who subdued Lions and served as a Prime Minister in Babylon
Ezekiel	Praise Him with **Ezekiel** a prophet and priest who served as God's messenger during Israel's captivity
Esther	Praise Him with **Esther** who won deliverance for her people
Ezra-Neh. 12:36	Praise Him with **Ezra**, a great scholar and scribe who led Israel out of captivity from Babylon to Jerusalem
Nehemiah	Praise Him with **Nehemiah** who brought spiritual reform to Israel and rebuilt the wall around Jerusalem in 52 days
Matt.-Jn.	Praise Him with **Mary** who gave birth to Jesus, the Messiah
Matt.-Jn.	Praise Him with **Joseph** who was the father of Jesus
Jn. 1; 3:22-36	Praise Him with **John the Baptist** the prophet who announced the coming of Christ
Matt.-Jn.	Praise Him with **Jesus** who is our Savior, King and Friend
1 & 2 Peter	Praise Him with **Peter,** a spokesman for the disciples
John	Praise Him with **John** who loved the Lord
Matt. - Jn.	Praise Him with the other **disciples**—Matthew, Mark, Andrew, James, Philip, Bartholomew, Thomas, Thaddaeus, and Judas—who served the Lord for three years
Jn. 11	Praise Him with **Lazarus** who was raised from the dead
Jn. 20	Praise Him with **Mary Magdalene** who was the first to see the resurrected Christ
Acts 6-7	Praise Him with **Stephen** who did great miracles and became the first martyr
Acts 7:58-28:31	Praise Him with **Paul** who was an apostolic teacher whose letters comprise much of the New testament
Acts 13	Praise Him with **Barnabus** who served God in the nations

Acts 15:22-19:10 Praise Him with **Silas** who was a leader in the church at Jerusalem and accompanied Paul on missionary journeys

Acts 16-28 Praise Him with **Luke** who was an educated man, physician and author of one of the Gospels and the Book of Acts

Heb. 12:1 Praise Him that we are surrounded by "so great a cloud of witnesses" that we may lay aside every weight and every sin, and run the race with endurance as we look to Jesus, the author and finisher of our faith

Chapter Thirteen

Praise Him Everywhere

*"Blessing and honor and glory and power
Be to Him who sits on the throne,
And to the Lamb, forever and ever!"*
Rev. 5:13

Praise Him Throughout Your Life

Jer. 1:4-5	Praise Him before you were formed in the womb
Ps. 139:14-15	Praise Him when you are conceived and formed in the womb
Ps. 71:6	Praise Him when you come out of your mother's womb (Job 1:21; Ps. 22:10)
Ps. 150:6	Praise Him when you have breath
Ps. 8:2	Praise Him when you are a baby (Matt. 21:16)
Ps. 8:2	Praise Him when you are a child (Matt. 21:15)
Ps. 148:12-13	Praise Him when you are young
Ps. 71:18	Praise Him when you are old
Ps. 104:33	Praise Him when you are alive (Ps. 146:2; Is. 39:19)
Ps. 102:20-21	Praise Him when you are appointed to die
Matt. 26:30	Praise Him when you face death (2Sam. 22:6-7)
1Cor. 15:55	Praise Him when He seizes all power from death
Ps. 56:13	Praise Him when you are delivered from death
Ez. 37:13	Praise Him when you have your graves opened
Jn. 11:39-44	Praise Him when you are raised from the dead (Jn. 12:17)
Ps. 22:26	Praise Him when you live for eternity (Ps. 45:17; 61:8)
Is. 25:8	Praise Him when He takes away death for all time

Praise Him In Every Place

Ps. 62:5	Praise Him alone
Ps. 34:3	Praise Him with me
Ps. 95:1-2	Praise Him with us
1Cor. 14:26	Praise Him together

Ps. 139:9	Praise Him when you are in the depths of the sea (Ps. 148:7)
Is. 58:14	Praise Him when you are on the high hills (Hab. 3:19)
Is. 42:11	Praise Him when you are in the highest mountains (Is. 44:23)
Ps. 72:9	Praise Him when you are in the wilderness
Ps. 148:7	Praise Him when you are in the earth
Ps. 48:10	Praise Him when you are in the ends of the earth (Is. 42:10)
Ps. 57:5-6	Praise Him when you are above the earth
Ps. 148:1	Praise Him when you are in the heights
Ps. 150:1	Praise Him when you are in His sanctuary
Ps. 89:5	Praise Him when you are in the heavens
Ps. 108:5	Praise Him when you are above the heavens

Ps. 35:18	Praise Him when you are among many people
Ps. 105:1	Praise Him when you are in the nations (Ps. 22:27; 57:9)
Ps. 109:30	Praise Him when you are among the multitudes
Ps. 138:1	Praise Him when you are before other gods
Ps. 111:1	Praise Him when you are in the congregation
Heb. 2:12	Praise Him when you are in the midst of the assembly
Ps. 22:25	Praise Him when you are in the great assembly
Philemon 4	Praise Him when you remember your brothers and sisters
Ps. 103:20-22	Praise Him when you minister before Him (1Chr. 6:4, 31-48)
1Chr. 15:16-29	Praise Him when you stand before the Ark (1Chr. 16:1-42)
Ps. 107:32	Praise Him when you are with the elders

Ps. 138:4	Praise Him when you are a king (Ps. 148:11; Dan. 4:34)
Ps. 148:11	Praise Him when you are a prince or a judge
Zech. 14:16-17	Praise Him when you go up to Jerusalem to worship (2Ki. 18:22)
Ps. 99:9	Praise Him when you come to His holy hill
Ps. 138:2	Praise Him when you worship before His holy temple
Ps. 5:7	Praise Him when you come into His temple
Ps. 100:4	Praise Him when you come into His gates (Jer. 7:2)
Ps. 100:4	Praise Him when you come into His courts
Ps. 135:2	Praise Him when you stand in the courts of the Lord
Song 2:4	Praise Him when you are in His banqueting house
Ps. 103:19	Praise Him when you are in His throne room (Rev. 4:2-10)
Job 38:22	Praise Him when you are in His treasure house (Ps. 135:7; 145:3; Is. 45:3; Jer. 10:13; 51:16)
Ps. 45:11, 15	Praise Him when you see the King (Es. 2:17; 5:2)
Ps. 99:5	Praise Him when you come to His footstool
Ps. 42:4	Praise Him when you are in the house of the Lord (Ps. 84:4)
Ps. 150:1	Praise Him when you are in His mighty firmament
Ps. 72:16	Praise Him when you flourish in His city
Ps. 92:13	Praise Him when you flourish in His courts

Praise Him In His Presence

Eccl. 8:12	Praise Him when you fear before Him
2Chr. 20:18	Praise Him when you bow before Him
2Ki. 20:3	Praise Him when you walk before Him
Ps. 68:4	Praise Him when you come before Him
2Chr. 29:11	Praise Him when you stand before Him
Ps. 42:2	Praise Him when you appear before Him
1 Sam. 2:18	Praise Him when you minister before Him
2Chr. 34:27	Praise Him when you humble yourself before Him (Jas. 4:10; 1Pet. 5:6)

Ps. 100:2	Praise Him when you come before His presence (face)
1Chr. 16:11	Praise Him when you seek His face (2Chr. 7:14; Ps. 24:6; 27:8; Song 2:14)
Lam. 2:19	Praise Him when you pour out your heart before His face
Job 22:26	Praise Him when you lift your face to Him
Ps. 17:15	Praise Him when you see His face
Ps. 89:14	Praise Him when mercy and truth are before His face
Ps. 80:19	Praise Him when His face shines on you (Ps. 67:1)
Dan. 9:17	Praise Him when His face shines on His sanctuary
Ps. 16:8	Praise Him when you set the Lord before your face (Ps. 41:12)
Dt. 5:4	Praise Him when you speak to Him face to face
1Cor. 13:12	Praise Him when you see Him face to face
1Cor. 3:18	Praise Him when you unveil your face before Him
Pr. 16:15	Praise Him when you find life before His face
Ezra 3:10-11	Praise Him when you build His house
Ezra 7:27	Praise Him when you beautify His house
Neh. 12:31	Praise Him when you stand on the wall of His house
Neh. 12:40	Praise Him when you stand in His house
Is. 52:8	Praise Him when you are a watchmen in His house (Is. 62:6-7)
Ps. 84:10	Praise Him when you are a doorkeeper of His house
1Chr. 16:4	Praise Him when you are a worshiper in His house
1Chr. 6:31	Praise Him when you are a singer in His house
1Chr. 25:6	Praise Him when you play music in His house
Ps. 89:7	Praise Him when you are in the assembly of saints
Is. 64:11	Praise Him when you are in the temple (Is. 66:6)
Is. 66:19	Praise Him when you are among the Gentiles (2Sam. 22:50; Rom. 15:9)
Dt. 32:4	Praise Him when you encounter Him as the Rock (1Sam. 2:2; 2Sam. 22:32; Ps. 18:31)
Ex. 33:21	Praise Him when you stand on the rock (Ps. 40:2)
Song 2:14	Praise Him when you are in the rock (Ob. 1:3)
Ps. 78:16, 20	Praise Him when water comes from the Rock
Ps. 81:16	Praise Him when honey comes from the Rock

2Sam. 22:2	Praise Him when your Rock is your fortress (Ps. 18:2; 31:2-3)
2Sam. 22:47	Praise Him when your Rock is your salvation (Ps. 62:6; 95:1)
Ps. 71:3	Praise Him when your Rock is your refuge (Ps. 94:22)
Is. 2:10	Praise Him when your Rock is your hiding place
1Cor. 10:4	Praise Him when your Rock is your source of water
Song 1:12	Praise Him when you are at the King's table
Ps. 23:5	Praise Him when He prepares a table for you in the presence of your enemies
Lu. 24:30	Praise Him when you come to the table of the Lord (Lu. 22:19; 1Cor. 11:24)
Jn. 6:11	Praise Him when you eat
Dan. 8:10	Praise Him when you eat and are satisfied (Ps. 63:5)
1 Cor. 10:16	Praise Him when you eat and drink in communion with Him (Acts 27:35)
Matt. 26:26-28	Praise Him when He becomes the bread and wine for you
Jn. 6:54	Praise Him when you eat and drink of Him and are raised up on the last day to eternal life
Matt. 6:11	Praise Him when He supplies your daily bread
Ps. 116:13	Praise Him for your cup of salvation
1Cor. 10:16	Praise Him for your cup of blessing
Ps. 23:5	Praise Him for your cup runs over
Ps. 46:10	Praise Him when you know Him in the stillness
1Chr. 28:9	Praise Him when you know Him by seeking Him
Hos. 6:3	Praise Him when you know Him by pressing in to Him
Jn. 14:17	Praise Him when you know Him because He lives in you
2Tim. 1:12	Praise Him when you know Him through trusting Him
1Jn. 4:8	Praise Him when you know Him through loving others
1Jn. 5:20	Praise Him when you know Him by living in Christ

Ps. 87:2	Praise Him when you are in the gates of the city (Is. 60:18)
Gen. 22:16-17	Praise Him when you possess the gates of the city
Neh. 12:31, 38	Praise Him when you are on the wall of the city
Josh. 6:1-19	Praise Him when you surround the city
Josh. 6:20-21	Praise Him when you conquer the city
Ps. 48:1	Praise Him when you are in the city
Matt. 5:14-16	Praise Him when you are the city
Ex. 3:2-6	Praise Him when you see Him in the burning bush
Gen. 18:1-2	Praise Him when you see Him from under a tree
Lu. 19:4-6	Praise Him when you see Him from up in a tree
	Praise Him when you see Him hanging on a tree
Ps. 1:3	Praise Him when you are like a tree planted by water
Ps 52:8	Praise Him when you are like a green Olive tree
Ps. 92:12	Praise Him when you are like a palm tree
Pr. 11:30; 15:4	Praise Him when you are like a fruitful tree of life
Is. 55:12	Praise Him when you are like a tree clapping hands
Is. 61:3	Praise Him when you are like a righteous oak
Hos. 14:6	Praise Him when you are like a cedar of Lebanon
Hos. 14:8	Praise Him when you are like a green pine tree
Matt. 7:18-19	Praise Him when you are like a good tree
Job 14:7-9	Praise Him when you are like a tree cut down yet sprout again

Chapter Fourteen

Praise Him With All Your Being

*All the angels stood around the throne and the elders
and the four living creatures, and fell on their faces
before the throne and worshiped God,
saying: "Amen! Blessing and glory and wisdom,
Thanksgiving and honor and power and might,
Be to our God forever and ever. Amen."*
Rev. 7:11-12

Praise Him With All That You Are And All You Have

Rom. 15:6	Praise Him with one mind
Rom. 15:6	Praise Him with one mouth
Ps. 71:14	Praise Him more and more
Ps. 54:6	Praise Him for it is good
Ps. 147:1	Praise Him for it is pleasant and beautiful
Ps. 9:1	Praise Him with your whole heart (Ps. 111:1; 119:10; 138:1)
Zeph. 3:14	Praise Him with all your heart (Matt. 22:27)
Dt. 6:5	Praise Him with all your soul
Lu. 10:27	Praise Him with all your mind
Ex. 15:2	Praise Him with all your strength
Ps. 103:1	Praise Him with all that is in you
2Sam. 6	Praise Him with undignified abandon
Rev. 5:12	Praise Him with a loud voice (Lu. 17:15; 19:37)
2Chr. 20:19	Praise Him with a very loud voice
Ezra 3:11	Praise Him with great shouts (Ps. 35:27)
Ps. 81:1	Praise Him with loud, joyful shouts (Ps. 33:3)
Matt. 21:9	Praise Him with loud "Hosannas"

Neh. 12:42	Praise Him loudly
Phil. 4:10	Praise Him greatly (Ps. 48:1; 71:23; 145:3)
2Chr. 30:21	Praise Him gladly
Heb. 4:16	Praise Him boldly
1Chr. 29:9	Praise Him wholeheartedly
Rom. 12:11	Praise Him enthusiastically
Ps. 40:16	Praise Him repeatedly
Ps. 70:4	Praise Him continually
2Chr. 29:30	Praise Him with gladness (Neh. 12:27)
2Chr. 30:21	Praise Him with great gladness
Jer. 33:11	Praise Him with joy and gladness (Chr. 29:30)
Ps. 63:5	Praise Him with joyful lips
Ps. 107:22	Praise Him with rejoicing
Ps. 69:30	Praise Him with thanksgiving
1Cor. 14:15	Praise Him with the spirit
Ps. 47:7	Praise Him with understanding (1Cor. 14:15)
Ps. 119:7	Praise Him with an upright heart
Phil. 1:11	Praise Him with fruits of righteousness
Col. 4:2	Praise Him with watchful prayers
Gen. 4:4	Praise Him when you bring your offering (Heb. 11:4)
Gen. 22:1-14	Praise Him when you offer Him everything (Heb. 11:17)
Mark 12:42-43	Praise Him when you bring Him an excellent offering
Ps. 96:8	Praise Him when you bring your offering into His courts
Ps. 119:108	Praise Him when you bring freewill offerings
Jud. 5:2	Praise Him when you offer yourself

Praise Him With All Your Heart

1Chr. 29:9	Praise Him when you have a loyal heart
Ps. 51:10	Praise Him when you have a clean heart
Ps. 51:17	Praise Him when you have a contrite heart
Ps. 64:10	Praise Him when you have an upright heart
Ps. 73:1	Praise Him when you have a pure heart
Ps. 101:2	Praise Him when you have a perfect heart
Ps. 61:2	Praise Him when your heart is overwhelmed
Ps. 73:26	Praise Him when your heart fails you

119

Ps. 109:22	Praise Him when your heart is wounded
Ps. 57:7	Praise Him when your heart is steadfast (Ps. 108:1)
Ps. 84:2	Praise Him when your heart cries out for Him
Ps. 73:26	Praise Him when He is the strength of your heart
Ps. 40:4	Praise Him when you trust Him and He blesses you
Ps. 125:1	Praise Him when you trust Him and become secure
Acts 10:43	Praise Him when you trust Him and He forgives you
Gal. 3:26	Praise Him when you trust Him and you become His child
Jn. 3:36	Praise Him when you trust Him and you have everlasting life (Jn. 6:47)
Ps. 46:10	Praise Him when you are still
Ps. 65:1	Praise Him when you are waiting for Him (Ps. 27:14)
Ps. 37:7	Praise Him when you are patient and rest in Him (Ps. 40:1)
Rom. 12:12	Praise Him when you are patient in tribulation (2Cor. 6:4)
Ps. 119:11	Praise Him when you have His Word in your heart
Ps. 139:23	Praise Him when He knows your heart

Praise Him With All Your Seeking And Desire

Ps. 40:16	Praise Him when you search for Him (Ps. 70:4)
Job 23:3-12	Praise Him when you cannot find Him (Song 5:6)
Dt. 4:29	Praise Him when you seek Him with all your heart and soul and then find Him (Is. 55:6; Jer. 29:13-14)
Jer. 29:13	Praise Him when you find Him near (Ps. 22:3; Is. 55:6)
Heb. 4:16	Praise Him when you draw near to Him (Heb. 10:19-22)
Jas. 4:8	Praise Him when He draws near to you
Is. 58:9	Praise Him when He says, "Here I am"
Ps. 56:10	Praise Him when you read the Word
Col. 3:16	Praise Him when you sing the Word
Is. 66:2, 5	Praise Him when you tremble at His Word
Job 23:12	Praise Him when you eat His Word (Ez. 3:1-3)

Matt. 6:9	Praise Him when He teaches you to pray
Phil. 4:6	Praise Him when you pray
Ps. 65:2	Praise Him when He hears your prayer (Ps. 120:1)
Mk. 11:22-24	Praise Him when you find faith in prayer
Is. 65:24	Praise Him when He answers before you pray
Ps. 61:5-8	Praise Him when He answers prayer (Is. 30:19; Ps. 91:15; 118:5; 143:1; 145:19; Jer. 29:12; Zech. 13:9; Matt. 7:7-8, 11; 21:12; Jn. 14:13-14; 15:7; 16:23-24; Jas. 5:15-16; 1Jn. 3:22; 5:14-16)
Ps. 19:9-10	Praise Him as you desire His laws
Ps. 27:4	Praise Him as you desire His courts
Ps. 34:12	Praise Him as you desire life
Ps. 73:25	Praise Him as you desire His presence
Pr. 3:15	Praise Him as you desire wisdom
Is. 26:8	Praise Him as you desire the glory of His name
Matt. 16:24	Praise Him as you desire to follow Him
Matt. 20:26-7	Praise Him as you desire greatness through servanthood
Lu. 9:24	Praise Him as you desire to lose your life
Lu. 10:24	Praise Him as you desire to see His wonders
Rom. 10:1	Praise Him as you desire for Israel to be saved
1Cor. 12:31	Praise Him as you desire God's best spiritual gifts
1Cor. 14:1, 39	Praise Him as you desire to prophesy
2Cor. 5:2	Praise Him as you desire your heavenly body
2Cor. 7:11	Praise Him as you desire holiness following repentance
Phil. 1:23	Praise Him as you desire to live and desire to be with the Lord
Rev. 22:17	Praise Him as you desire the water of life
Ps. 27:4	Praise Him as you desire one thing—His presence
2Chr. 1:8-10	Praise Him as you ask for one thing—wisdom
Mark 10:21	Praise Him as you sell out for one thing—following Jesus
Lu. 10:4	Praise Him as you choose one thing—worship
Phil. 3:13	Praise Him as you do one thing—press on to know Him

Praise Him With All Your Excellence

Ps. 66:1	Praise Him when you make His praise joyful
Ps. 66:2	Praise Him when you make His praise glorious
Ps. 66:8	Praise Him when you make His praise heard
Jer. 30:19	Praise Him when you make His praise merry

Ps. 33:2	Praise Him when you make melodies for Him
Eph. 5:19	Praise Him when you make melody in your heart to the Lord
Ps. 45:17	Praise Him when you make His name to be remembered (Ps. 105:1)

Ps. 26:7	Praise Him with the voice of thanksgiving
Ps. 42:4	Praise Him with the voice of joy
Ps. 47:1	Praise Him with the voice of triumph
Is. 51:3	Praise Him with the voice of melody
Jer. 33:11	Praise Him with the voice of the Bridegroom
Jer. 33:11	Praise Him with the voice of the Bride
Rev. 19:1, 6	Praise Him with the voice of a multitude

Ps. 27:6	Praise Him with the sacrifice of Joy
Ps. 51:16-17	Praise Him with the sacrifice of a broken spirit
Ps. 51:19	Praise Him with the sacrifice of righteousness
Ps. 54:6	Praise Him with the sacrifice of praise (Jer. 33:11; Heb. 13:15)
Ps. 116:17	Praise Him with the sacrifice of thanksgiving
Rom. 12:1	Praise Him with the sacrifice of our bodies
Heb. 13:15-16	Praise Him with the sacrifice of true fellowship and sharing

Praise Him With All Your Ability

Jn. 4:24	Praise Him and worship in spirit and in truth
Ps. 99:9	Praise Him and worship Him for He is holy

Ps. 27:14	Praise Him when you wait on the Lord (Is. 40:31)
Ps. 52:9	Praise Him when you wait on His name

Ps. 71:23	Praise Him when you sing
Ezra 3:13	Praise Him when you weep
Ps. 95:6	Praise Him when you kneel
Ps. 47:1	Praise Him when you shout
Ps. 71:24	Praise Him when you speak
Ps. 149:3	Praise Him when you dance
Ps. 65:1	Praise Him when you are silent
Job 37:14	Praise Him when you stand still
Ps. 95:6	Praise Him when you bow down
Ps. 20:5	Praise Him when you lift a banner
Acts 3:8	Praise Him when you walk and leap
Ps. 63:4	Praise Him when you lift your hands
Ps. 47:1	Praise Him when you clap your hands
Is. 42:10	Praise Him when you sing a new song
Ps. 134:1	Praise Him when you stand before Him
Ps.150:3-5	Praise Him when you play an instrument
Job 22:26-27	Praise Him when you lift your face to Him
2Chr. 7:3; 20:18	Praise Him when you put your face on the ground
Matt. 21:7	Praise Him when you throw your coats before Him
Rev. 4:10	Praise Him when you cast your crowns before Him
Rev. 7:9	Praise Him when you wave palm branches before Him
Gen. 4:21	Praise Him with the flute/organ (harp)
Ex. 15:20	Praise Him with the timbrels (drum) (Ps. 68:25)
Ex. 28:33-36	Praise Him with the bells (Ex. 39:25-26)
Josh. 6:4	Praise Him with the ram's horn
2Sam. 6:5	Praise Him with the tambourine
2Sam. 6:5	Praise Him with the castanets
2Sam. 6:5	Praise Him with the cymbals
Ps. 150:5	Praise Him with the high cymbals
Ps. 150:5	Praise Him with loud cymbals
2Chr. 7:6	Praise Him with the trumpet
Ps. 33:2	Praise Him with the harp (Gen. 4:21; Ps. 71:22)
Ps. 33:2	Praise Him with an instrument of ten strings
Ps. 57:8	Praise Him with the psaltery (lute)
Ps. 149:3	Praise Him with timbrel and harp
Ps. 150:4	Praise Him with trumpet, lute, stringed instruments and flutes

Ps. 149:3	Praise Him with dancing
Ps. 28:7	Praise Him with your song
Ps. 95:2	Praise Him with psalms (PS. 98:5)
2Chr. 29:30	Praise Him as you sing and worship with the words of David
2Sam. 22:50	Praise Him when you sing of His name
Heb. 2:11-12	Praise Him when He sings of His name
1Chr. 16:9	Praise Him when you talk of His wonders
Mal. 3:16	Praise Him when you meditate on His name
Ps. 71:23	Praise Him when you extol Him with your lips
Ps. 66:17	Praise Him when you extol Him with your tongue
Acts 2:11	Praise Him when you speak in tongues the wonderful works of God
Pr. 15:4	Praise Him when your tongue becomes a tree of life (Pr. 18:21)
Pr. 10:11	Praise Him when your righteous mouth is a well of life
Is. 12:3	Praise Him when you draw water from wells of salvation
Gen. 2:7	Praise Him when He gives you breath
Job 12:10	Praise Him when He holds your breath in His hand
Ps. 150:6	Praise Him everything that has breath
Ps. 44:8	Praise Him when you boast of His name
Ps. 84:10	Praise Him when you boast of His presence
Gal. 6:14	Praise Him when you boast of Him (Ps. 34:2. 44:8; 1Cor. 1:31)

Praise Him With All Your Joy

Neh. 8:10	Praise Him when the joy of the Lord is your strength
Hab. 3:17-18	Praise Him when you have joy even when you are facing great adversity
Ps. 16:11	Praise Him when you find the fullness of joy in His presence
Is. 51:11	Praise Him when you obtain everlasting joy (Is. 35:10; 61:7)
Is. 55:12	Praise Him when you go out with joy and peace
Ps. 126:5-6	Praise Him when you reap with joy
Ps. 89:15, 16	Praise Him when you walk in the light of His countenance and rejoice all day
1Pet. 1:8	Praise Him when you rejoice with unspeakable joy
Jude 1:24	Praise Him when you stand faultless before Him with exceeding joy
Jn. 15:11	Praise Him when His joy is in you
Jn. 15:11	Praise Him when your joy is full
Acts 2:28	Praise Him when you are full of joy
Ps. 5:11	Praise Him with shouts of joy
Is. 65:14	Praise Him with songs of joy (Ps. 118:15)
Ps. 37:4	Praise Him when you delight yourself in Him. He will give you the desires of your heart
Ps. 37:5	Praise Him when you commit your ways to Him. He will reveal your righteousness and justice
Pr. 3:5-6	Praise Him when you trust in Him. He will direct your paths

Praise Him With All The Songs And Hymns In The Bible

Ex. 15:1-21	Praise Him with a song of victory over Pharaoh's army
Num. 21:17	Praise Him with a song of thanks for His provision
Dt. 32:1-43	Praise Him with a song of thanks for His covenants and compassion for His people
Jud. 5:2-31	Praise Him with a song of triumph over enemies
1Sam. 18:7	Praise Him with a song of the defeat of God's enemies

2Sam. 22:2-51	Praise Him with a song of praise after He rescues you from all your enemies
1Chr. 16:8-36	Praise Him with a song of joy for His faithfulness and when His presence (the ark) is in your midst
2Chr. 20:21-22	Praise Him with a song of praise as you defeat overwhelming odds
Ezra 3:11	Praise Him with a song of exaltation for His mercies endure forever
Song of Songs	Praise Him with a song of love between the Bride and the Bridegroom
Psalms	Praise Him with a song of overcoming and delight through every circumstance and emotion in life
Is. 5:1-30	Praise Him with a song of the Beloved's vineyard
Is. 12:1-6	Praise Him with a song of appreciation for His salvation
Is. 26:1-21	Praise Him with a song of appreciation for His righteousness, mercy and justice
Is. 42:10-17	Praise Him with a song of celebration for His power and might
Lamentations	Praise Him with a song of mourning for the destruction of Jerusalem and hope for her restoration
Hab. 3:1-15	Praise Him with a song of awe for His majesty
Lu. 1:46-55	Praise Him with a song of adoration for His faithfulness and greatness
Rev. 5:9-13	Praise Him with a song of the Lamb—lauding His redemption, finished work and adoring His worthiness
Rev. 15:3-4	Praise Him with a song of Moses and the song of the Lamb calling for all nations to worship before Him

Praise Him As You Lift Him Up

Jn. 12:32	Praise Him when you lift Him up
2Sam. 22:49	Praise Him when He lifts you up (Ps. 18:48; Jas. 4:10)
Is. 33:3	Praise Him when you lift yourself up
Is. 33:10	Praise Him when He lifts Himself up

Job 22:26	Praise Him when you lift your face to Him
Num. 6:26	Praise Him When He lifts His countenance on you
Ps. 28:2	Praise Him when you lift up your hands
	(Ps. 63:4; 134:2)
Ps. 10:12	Praise Him when He lifts His hand
Ps. 20:5	Praise Him when you lift up a banner
Is. 5:26	Praise Him when He lifts up a banner
Ps. 24:7, 9	Praise Him when you lift up your head (Lu. 21:28)
Ps. 25:1	Praise Him when you lift up your soul (Ps. 86:4)
Job 38:34	Praise Him when you lift your voice (Is. 40:9)
Ps. 121:1	Praise Him when you lift up your eyes (Jn. 4:35)
Lam. 3:41	Praise Him when you lift up your heart
Ps. 9:13	Praise Him when He lifts you from death
Jn. 12:32	Praise Him when He is lifted up in death (Jn. 3:14)
Is. 6:1	Praise Him when He is high and lifted up

Chapter Fifteen

Praise Him At All Times

"Amen! Blessing and glory and wisdom,
Thanksgiving and honor and power and might,
Be to our God forever and ever. Amen."
Rev. 7:12

Ex. 19:16	Praise Him for we see His glory in the morning
Ex. 16:7-12	Praise Him for He provides us with manna in the morning
Ps. 113:2	Praise Him from this time forth and forever more (Ps. 115:18; 131:3)
Ps. 121:4	Praise Him for He preserves your going out and coming in from this time forth and forever more
Ps. 125:2	Praise Him for He surrounds His people just like the mountains surround Jerusalem from this time forth and forever more
Ps. 131:3	Praise Him and hope in Him from this time forth and forever more
Is. 59:21	Praise Him for He has put His words in our mouths and in the mouths of our descendants from this time forth and forever more
Es. 4:14	Praise Him for you are in the kingdom for such a time as this
Song 2:12	Praise Him for it is the time of singing
Hos. 10:12	Praise Him for it is time to seek the Lord until He comes
Jn. 4:23	Praise Him for it is the time to worship the Father in spirit and in truth
Jn. 12:23	Praise Him for it is the time for Jesus to be glorified

1Chr. 16:36	Praise Him from everlasting to everlasting
Ps. 145:4	Praise Him from generation to generation
1 Cor. 3:18	Praise Him from glory to glory
Rom. 1:17	Praise Him from faith to faith
Zech. 9:9	Praise Him when your King comes to you
Ps. 47:5-7	Praise Him when your King rises in the earth with a shout
Eccl. 3:1-11	Praise Him for His perfect timing in all things
Ps. 102:13	Praise Him when it is the time for His favor
Is. 12:1	Praise Him when He is angry with you and He turns His anger away and comforts you
2Chr. 8:14	Praise Him when it is your duty
Ps. 73:25	Praise Him when it is your desire
2Chr. 17:6	Praise Him when it is your delight (Ps. 37:4)
Ps. 16:3	Praise Him when He delights in you
Ps. 130:6	Praise Him when you watch for the morning
Ex. 14:24	Praise Him when you keep the morning watch (Ps. 5:3; Matt. 14:25)
Jud. 7:19	Praise Him when you keep the middle watch
Ps. 63:6	Praise Him when you keep the night watches (Ps. 119:148; 134:1; Lam. 2:19; Mk. 6:48)
2Chr. 23:4, 6	Praise Him when you keep watch in the Lord's house
Pr. 8:34	Praise Him when you keep watch at the King's gate
Hab. 2:1	Praise Him when you keep watch over God's people (Mk. 13:33-37)
Ps. 81:3	Praise Him when it is the time of the new moon
Ps. 102:13	Praise Him when it is the time of His promised favor

Ps. 72:5	Praise Him as long as the sun and moon endure
Ps. 119:147	Praise Him before the dawning of the morning
Ps. 57:8	Praise Him when you waken the dawn
Ps. 108:2	Praise Him when it is dawn
1Chr. 23:30	Praise Him when it is morning (Ps. 59:16)
Ps. 113:3	Praise Him when the sun comes up
Ps. 55:17	Praise Him when it is noon
Ps. 42:8	Praise Him when it is evening (Ps. 92:2)
Ps. 141:2	Praise Him when you bring the evening sacrifice
Ps. 113:3	Praise Him when the sun goes down (Mal. 1:11)
Ps. 119:62	Praise Him when it is midnight (Acts 16:25)

Ps. 118:24	Praise Him for this is the day that He has made
Ex. 20:11	Praise Him on the Sabbath
Acts 20:27	Praise Him on the first day of the week

Ps. 61:8	Praise Him daily
Dan. 6:10	Praise Him three times a day
Ps. 119:164	Praise Him seven times a day
Ps. 44:8	Praise Him all day (Ps. 71:8; 89:16)
Ps. 145:2	Praise Him every day (2Chr. 30:21)
Is. 66:23	Praise Him from month to month
Is. 66:23	Praise Him from week to week
Ps. 34:1	Praise Him continually (Ps. 35:27; Heb. 13:15)
1Thess. 2:13	Praise Him without ceasing
Phil. 4:4	Praise Him always (Eph. 5:20; 1Thess. 5:16)

Ps. 34:1	Praise Him whenever (Rev. 4:9)
1Tim. 2:8	Praise Him wherever (2Cor. 2:14)
1Cor. 10:31	Praise Him whatever (Phil. 4:8; Col. 3:17)
Ps. 50:23	Praise Him whoever (2Cor. 10:17; 1Jo. 4:15)
Ps. 52:9	Praise Him forever (Ps. 61:8; 75:9)

1Thess. 5:16-18*Rejoice always, pray without ceasing, in everything give thanks; for this is the will of God in Christ Jesus for you.*

Hallelujah! Amen!

What in heaven or earth can stop us from praising God when we are faced with these verses? What reason do any of us have to keep silent in the light of His wonders? Where can you even begin to find a worthy cause that can keep you from passionate praises?

Paul also asks us if there is anything that can separate us from Christ (Rom. 8:35). He answers His own question—there is nothing small or great that can keep us from His most wonderful love and presence— not even death, itself, can keep us from Him or from the torrent of praise that must surely arise from our hearts and lives.

Praise Him!

What a fool I was—I thought for a brief moment that I could complete this task of listing all the reasons to praise Him. In fact, His greatness is totally unsearchable:

Ps. 145:3 *Great is the Lord, and greatly to be praised; And His greatness is unsearchable.*

Job 5:9 *Who does great things, and unsearchable, Marvelous things without number.*

Job 8:10 *He does great things past finding out, Yes, wonders without number.*

Ps. 106:2 *Who can utter the mighty acts of the Lord? Who can declare all His praise?*

Rom. 11:33 *Oh, the depth of the riches both of the wisdom and knowledge of God! How unsearchable are His judgments And His ways past finding out!*

Eph. 3:8 *To me, who am less than the least of all the saints, this grace was given, that I should preach among the Gentiles the unsearchable riches of Christ.*

The longer I worked on this little book, the faster the ideas came for different times, places and reasons we have to praise the Lord. I realized that there were not enough libraries in the entire world to carry the books that would be needed to comprehensively cover the multitude of reasons to offer Him praise. I realized that if every human being began right now to continuously praise Him, they would never exhaust the host of praises that were due to the Lord—not if they sang and spoke of His wonders for a year; ten years; one thousand years; eternity!

His greatness will never cease and His deeds will go on necessitating their due honor for eternity.

Jn. 21:25 *And there are also many other things that Jesus did, which if they were written one by one, I suppose that even the world itself could not contain the books that would be written. Amen.*

Praise Him!

The Psalmist said:

Ps. 57:10 (Ps. 36:5) *For Your mercy reaches unto the heavens, And Your truth (faithfulness) unto the clouds.*

He was attempting to give some form of measurement to the mercy, truth and faithfulness of the Lord. In his mind, he had declared an immeasurable distance, as he thought that no man could ever reach the clouds. Now, here we are today, and men are able to go into outer space and millions of people fly above the clouds every day. It is quite impossible to calculate the greatness of the Lord, and there is no way to account for all His goodness.

So, I ask you to continue these chapters in your own heart. May massive choruses of praise ascend from you day and night—no matter what trials, hardships, pressures or difficulties face you; lift your heart in praise to the Lord who is always very near.

Praise Him!

In his devotional "Strengthen My Spirit." Charles Spurgeon comments on this verse:

Ps. 71:14 *But I will hope continually, and will yet praise Thee more and more.*

> *When sin conquered the realm of manhood, it slew all the minstrels except those of the race of Hope. For humanity, amid all its sorrows and sins, hope sings on. To believers in Jesus, there remains a royal race of bards, for we have a hope of glory, a lively hope, a hope eternal and divine. Because our hope abides, our praise continues.*

May hope, faith and devotion propel you to praise Him more and more. May He become your breath and your song. May praises create the fragrance of His presence in you and the light of His glory through you.

Praise Him!

Ex. 15:2 *The Lord is my strength and song, And He has become my salvation; He is my God, and I will **praise Him**; My father's God, and I will exalt Him.*

Ps. 22:23 *You who fear the LORD, **praise Him**! All you descendants of Jacob, glorify Him, And fear Him, all you offspring of Israel!*

THE WORSHIP ARTS CONSERVATORY

The Worship Arts Conservatory was commissioned in 1999 as an on-line school to aid worship ministers and Christian artists in the pursuit of a deeper knowledge of God while learning to use their art for His glory. We draw our expert faculty from local churches as well as from internationally renowned ministries to provide the specific training needed.

Founder and President Vivien Hibbert brings over twenty-five years of practical experience in the field of Worship Arts to our program and her leadership ensures that both our mission and values are articulated and transmitted to all constituencies.

Our current program offerings include our Associate of Worship Arts (A.W.A.) degree program and the Independent Study program. Course titles include: Worship Leading; Theology of the Psalms; Biblical Basis for Art; Fine Arts Vision & Administration; Prophetic Song; Prophetic Worship; Foundations for Leadership; Ministry Ethics; Theology of Worship; Worship Trends in Our Current Culture; Leadership; The Presence of God; Prayer and Meditation; The Tabernacle of David and many others.*

If you are interested in learning more about The Worship Arts Conservatory please email or visit:

info@worshiparts.org • www.worshiparts.org

Visit our bookstore for Vivien Hibbert's book, *Prophetic Worship*, her instrumental CD, *Shepherd's Suite*, and a variety of Native American flutes: www.worshiparts.org/html/wacshop.html

*Course Chart, Syllabi and Catalogue information is available online at www.worshiparts.org